LIFE
IS A RIDE

My Unconventional Journey of Cancer Recovery

Chris Joseph

Praise for Chris Joseph

"In the United States, holes in the medical system and blinders worn by doctors can turn any patient's healing journey into a perilous obstacle course. In *Life is a Ride*, Chris Joseph draws a map from one devastating diagnosis to empowered wellness, documenting some of the routes patients can take around the worst obstacles. A book of hope for anyone feeling daunted by the path in front of them."

    -Kimberly Kaye, FMHC and patient advocate

"Heartwarming, funny and engaging, Chris Joseph gives us one of the best kept secrets of being a successful cancer patient: take action and become the CEO of your own medical path! Everyone—doctors, patients, friends and family—can benefit from reading this honest, deep and moving book packed with good stories and tips."

    -Pamela Varady, PsyD

"We are taught in (pharma-funded) medical school there are three things we can do: cut, burn or toxin it out. It's a one-size-fits-all approach when in reality, each human being is unique and capable of healing. Chris is a true testament to this and I am so grateful to him for teaching me and allowing me to be a part of his healing journey. Cancer in one way or another has affected us all and it's high time we change our approach."

    -Melanie Gisler, DO, integrative family physician

Launch Pad Publishing 2020
launchpadpub.com

ISBN-13: 978-1-951407-29-2
ISBN-13: 978-1-951407-28-5 (ebook)

The author has tried to recreate events, locales and conversations from his memories of them. In order to maintain their anonymity, in a few cases he has changed the names of individuals and places.

This book is not intended as a substitute for health or medical advice. The reader should consult with a healing or medical professional in matters relating to their health, particularly with respect to any symptoms that may require immediate diagnosis or medical attention.

Foreword

I began coaching Chris Joseph in March 2017. He was an intelligent, successful and creative man in the prime of his life who was suddenly facing a major crisis. Chris had been diagnosed with stage III pancreatic cancer, an aggressive disease with the highest mortality rate of all major cancers.

Chris contacted me after reading my book *Warrior Pose*, a memoir of my own battle with stage IV cancer a decade earlier. I had been a network news foreign correspondent, fairly jaded and cynical from covering major wars around the world, and never dreamed that one day I would immerse myself in what the Western world considers "alternative medicine." That immersion saved my life and led me to a new career practicing Ayurvedic medicine and the ancient healing practices of yoga science.

In the beginning, Chris was physically weakened and emotionally distraught. He was losing faith in our allopathic system of medicine and felt disempowered and no longer in control of his own destiny. I could, however, sense a strong desire deep within him to reclaim his power and take charge of his situation no matter what the outcome might be.

I asked Chris if he was truly willing to make major, long-term changes to his diet, his lifestyle and his mental attitude. This, I told him, would be the only way I could help him. He committed himself to it, and thus we began a six-month journey designed to maximize his healing potential. Although it's never easy, Chris embraced the guidance with discipline and devotion, and began changing his life in almost every way. He took a hero's journey and has now become an inspiration to others facing cancer and life crises.

I remember at one point during our work together, when Chris was feeling low and uncertain, I told him I believed one day he would "pay it forward" by writing a book to inspire others through sharing his experience. That book has now come to fruition, and I'm honored that Chris asked me to write this foreword. I know that his powerful and inspirational story will touch your soul.

Brad Willis

Introduction

It starts with a first breath, and then with a cry.
It ends with a last breath on the day you die.
And in between life is a ride.

In late October of 2016, I was diagnosed with stage III pancreatic cancer. I thought I was fucked.

This is my story of dealing with the physical and emotional fallout of a cancer diagnosis. It's a story of tremendous fear. Of deep emotional pain. Of anguish, wondering how soon I was going to die and how painful my death would be.

And it's also a story of courage while fighting fear. Of independence. Of putting one foot in front of the other. Of daring to be different and not following conventional wisdom.

Of perseverance.

It's a story of connection. Of love. Of redemption. Of getting knocked down and finding a way to pick myself up off the mat.

Of hope.

And, most of all, it's a story of beating the odds and getting healthy.

There will be some heroes mentioned in the book. Those who are heroes get identified with their real names. These are the people who helped save my life. They include family, friends, folks in the medical profession and people who'd survived a brutal cancer diagnosis.

And there are also, to be generous, some goats. Villains. Every story has to have some villains, yes? Well, I've changed the names of some of the villains and goats in this book. I don't wish to publicly call them out for their bad advice, poor behavior, misdiagnoses or overall bad juju. (But contact me privately and I'll tell you who they are.) I don't wish them any ill will. They have to live with their bad behavior. That's punishment enough for me.

What this book is not:

This is not an advice book or a how-to manual. If I have learned anything over the last four years, it's that every one of us is different: our bodies, our genetics, our mental/emotional makeups, our personalities and our physical conditions.

There are different cancers, treatments, different locations in the body where cancer can live and various stages of cancer.

There are differences in insurance coverages, doctors and hospitals.

Some people have better immune systems than others. Some are battling other underlying conditions, which can make it more difficult to ward off cancer. Some people have more success with certain treatments than others. Some have more failures.

There is only one Chris Joseph, just as there is only one of you. The treatments that worked for me may not work for you. The treatments that failed me may very well work for you.

Please do not use this book expecting anything other than for it to be interesting, thought-provoking and ultimately life-affirming.

This book is broken into three parts and an epilogue that roughly correspond to the chronology of my story over the past four years. Occasionally, the chronological flow will be interrupted by an event, an anecdote or a short profile that relates to the book's themes.

Thank you in advance for reading.
Life is a ride.
Indeed.

The First Four Months

ONE

The Journey Begins

A man who introduced himself as a radiologist entered the room where I had been nervously sitting and fidgeting impatiently for more than 30 minutes. With a solemn face and a seemingly sad voice he bluntly said, "Sorry to give you the bad news…we found a mass in your pancreas."

Whatever he told me after that, I didn't hear. It was as if someone had hit the mute button. All I could see was that he was still talking, but there wasn't any sound coming out of his mouth.

He came unmuted at the end to say, "Talk to Doctor Mossgale. You can go home."

A routine visit to get some medical tests had turned into a calamity.

* * *

It started as an innocent and typical Southern California sunny day. A Monday. The 31st of October, Halloween Day. 2016.

I was 59. In a little less than two months, I would be turning the big six-oh.

I am a single dad and share custody of my boys. So that Monday morning was like most other school mornings. I woke my kids up, made sure they were fed, got them off to their school and then started my workday. After school and into the early evening, I was scheduled to take my boys to their respective Halloween gatherings with their friends, and after that, stay at home and give candy to trick-or-treaters.

My kids, Jasper and AJ, were 14 and 12 at the time. Both attended John Adams Middle School here in Santa Monica. Jasper was in eighth grade and AJ had just started middle school as a sixth-grader.

For all of that October and the latter part of September, I had been experiencing some abdominal discomfort. I was not in any pain, so I figured it was a lingering stomach bug. It seemed to bother me more at night, which I was puzzled about but didn't think much of at the time. The discomfort was nagging me, but it certainly didn't scream to me that something was seriously wrong. Finally, in late October, I decided to have it checked by Dr. Mossgale.

I had also, for maybe three to four months before this fateful day, been suffering from some major depression. This was strange because my life was pretty good. Work was thriving, my girlfriend, Susie, and I had righted the ship after a hiccup the year before and my kids were doing well.

I had no apparent reason to be depressed during this period, particularly this deeply despondent. For several weeks, there were many times I had contemplated ending my life. I couldn't figure out why I felt this way, and I was too depressed and too ashamed of being depressed to tell anyone or to seek help.

I made no connection between the depression and what I thought was a stomach virus.

Anyway, on Thursday, October 28, I visited Dr. Mossgale. He ordered some blood work for the lab, probed around my stomach and abdomen and then suggested I get some scans "to make sure everything is okay." What he didn't tell me was he felt something in my abdomen during his examination. He suggested I get a CT scan and an ultrasound and wrote a prescription for me.

In the mid-afternoon of that Halloween Day, I drove by myself to the imaging center in Santa Monica, not far from my house.

La-di-da. I wasn't worried at all. I'd had so many scans and ultrasounds over the course of my life—for my back, my shoulder, my colon—that I'd lost count.

I was still convinced that I had nothing more than a lingering virus and that with the passage of time and maybe some supplements and temporary dietary changes, I would be healed.

After the ultrasound, I waited for the second test. And waited. And waited. Longer than a "normal" wait. Thirty to 40 minutes went by.

Getting restless and impatient, I asked the front desk person what was going on. She went back and talked to someone, then came back and told me the first of many unforgettable things I heard that day.

"We need to contact your regular doctor because we want to run some additional tests that he didn't order."

Well, that wasn't good. I could feel my heart pounding.

Finally, the imaging staff ushered me in for whatever additional tests they wanted to run along with the CT scan I'd been waiting for.

After those tests, they had me wait. Again. This time, I was in a private room. Maybe another 30 minutes went by.

It seemed like an eternity.

I knew something was up, and I remember texting Susie that I was nervous. This was out of the realm of normal.

Susie.

At the age of 54, newly single after ending a 10-year marriage, I had hesitantly signed up for OK Cupid.

For a year and a half, I went on about two dozen first dates with all sorts of women. A few were interested in me. I was interested in a few of them. But nothing panned out.

Then lightning struck.

I clicked on Susie's OK Cupid profile one Saturday in October 2012 while I was at my office trying to catch up on work. Her looks were definitely intriguing. She came across as smart and literate. A part of her profile contained the lyrics of a Talking Heads song. I knew right away that we would have at least two big things in common—reading and music.

After a few messages and then a few phone calls, we agreed to meet. On our first date, we talked for hours and learned we had a lot in common. We'd both grown up in the San Fernando Valley. We were both the youngest siblings in our families. Most importantly, we could make each other laugh.

About 90 minutes in, Susie got up to go to the bathroom. As I watched her walk away from me in a gorgeous but oh-so-simple orange and white striped sundress, I realized I was completely taken with her.

When she came back to the table, I said something to her that I had never said to anyone on a first date.

"You are lovely."

* * *

At the imaging center soon after I texted Susie, the radiologist walked in with his seemingly sad face and his bad news, and after hearing "mass in your pancreas" and going deaf, I left.

I departed not knowing much. I didn't know if it was cancer, though I assumed it was. I didn't know how big it was. I didn't know if it meant I had tumors elsewhere in my body. I didn't know how serious it was and I didn't know what to do. The only thing I knew was that they found this thing—a mass—in my pancreas.

I went into full-bore panic. And fear. It was a fear that I had never experienced before. I was having trouble breathing.

I stepped into my car and started crying hysterically. It was about 3 pm and I needed to get home to take my boys to their respective Halloween functions. My ex-wife, Carmen, was visiting her boyfriend in Australia, so I couldn't ask her to help with the kids.

First, I called Susie. I was sobbing as I told her the news. Susie was stunned, I could tell. She didn't know what to say.

What could she say? When most of us hear anything about pancreatic cancer, we think it's a death sentence. So much so that it's the go-to cancer screenwriters use when they want to write a character out of a show. I'd seen that story told on the screen way too many times. Why is it the cancer of choice for killing off a character? The five-year survival rate for people with pancreatic cancer is 10 percent, according to the Pancreatic Cancer Network.

As Susie grappled with what she had just learned, she tried to calm me down with her very soothing voice and calm demeanor. "Well, you don't know what this means," she said. "We need to talk with your doctor. Maybe it's not as serious as it sounds."

But her words didn't work. I wasn't just beside myself; I was behind myself. Inconsolable. Panicked. I told Susie that I was pulling up my driveway and that I needed to hang up the phone and go in the house to talk with my children.

Before I stepped out of my car, I called Carmen. Because she was in a different country, and because of the international cell plan she was on, we needed to FaceTime to communicate.

As soon as she answered, I burst into tears again. But this was a bit different than my conversation with Susie. Carmen immediately saw that I was very upset and crying. Instantly, I could see that she was scared and assumed she thought maybe something had happened to one of our kids.

Sensing Carmen's fear, I said, "It's me, it's me!"

And then I told her what was going on. She, too, was stunned. "Should I come home?" she asked. I didn't know what to tell her. I actually don't even remember now if she cut her trip short or not, though I think she may have.

The calls with Susie and Carmen were so difficult.

As I got out of the car and took the short walk to the front door of my house, I was thinking a million thoughts, none good. First, I thought of my dad. He had been diagnosed with lung cancer in late 1985 and was dead less than four months later.

I wasn't even sure I was going to survive four months.

My mind was racing at lightning speed. How much money would I have to leave for my girlfriend, my ex-wife and my kids? How would I get my affairs in order? Who would I call? What would I tell my employees? My friends? The world?

I was utterly overwhelmed. And completely alone.

I was also obsessed with trying to figure out what I was going to tell the boys. I couldn't stop crying. I was in such fear. I couldn't just fake it and act like nothing was going on. At the same time, I didn't want to scare them. So I decided to give them just an overview.

I knew there was no way I was going to be able to keep it together in front of them.

I walked into my house and the boys and I quickly gathered together. I told them what I knew, but I gave them an edited version. And I was sobbing when I told them. I held their hands. And then they started crying. They saw and heard my pain and fear.

I tried to reassure them that I thought everything was going to be okay even though I didn't believe it myself. I thought I was a goner.

Telling my boys was the most difficult conversation of my entire life.

Later that night, I received a call from Dr. Mossgale. The radiologist had sent him the scan results. Dr. Mossgale said he would give me recommendations for oncologists the next day. When I asked him what I could or should do in the interim, he said yet another unforgettable thing I heard that day.

"Chris, I think you need to pray."

I was like, *What the fuck!?!?!?!*

What I learned a few weeks later was that Dr. Mossgale knew about as much as I did that night: that I had a tumor, a mass in my pancreas. He didn't know the type, the severity or anything else.

But let me tell you: when Dr. Mossgale suggested that I

pray, I was even more convinced that I wouldn't be around much longer. I thought I was done. Cooked. Toast.

And I was experiencing a paralyzing fear of suffering a painful, too-soon-to-die death combined with the sadness that I was not going to live long enough to see my kids grow up.

My cancer adventure had begun.

TWO

Some Background

Very early on in my cancer journey, I started writing a blog. Every few days, I would post my thoughts on Word-Press and email them to my friends and family.

I was so scared when I was diagnosed, but I knew almost right away that I didn't want to keep my condition a secret. And I wanted to feel less isolated because, for those first few days after receiving the news, I felt painfully alone. As my great friend, Michael O., a cancer survivor, put it: "Writing takes some of the loneliness out of the experience."

I knew that this was an experience like no other in my life. Nothing else came close.

In the years before my diagnosis, I had finally been learning to let love into my life. The gist of it was this: in many ways, I'd raised myself emotionally. I'd had to do this for various reasons, but in so doing, I shut people out in an effort to "protect" myself from getting hurt. This coping mechanism went on well into my adulthood.

A lot of people know that essentially, I'm a loner. I mean, I loved being in a relationship, and I loved being with my kids and my friends, but I also craved alone time. And in being protective, along with being a loner, I'd managed to push many people away over the decades.

Well, getting a cancer diagnosis was a game-changer. It was no time to be alone.

It was no time to be protective of my feelings or to push people away. It just wasn't.

I knew immediately that the mere act of blogging about my cancer experience was a way of letting people in on what I was feeling and experiencing. I knew it would be therapeutic, but I had no idea how it would be received by anyone who read what I wrote.

But I forged ahead anyway. And I received very moving and wonderful feedback from the first blog on. Anyone who knew my fragile state and didn't like what I was writing or who thought I was oversharing was likely not going to tell me.

In November 2016, when I was floundering, struggling to keep my head above water, grasping at straws and looking for positives, receiving immediate positive feedback on the blog helped me stay afloat.

I also let my blog readers know that if at any time they wanted to stop receiving blog emails for whatever reason, they could just email and let me know. I wouldn't be hurt. That much. Since I was in therapy, I could just add that to the list of grievances and issues that I still needed to work on. My therapist, Pamela, would be happy.

THREE

Oncologist Number One

The same doctor who told me I should pray, Dr. Mossgale, gave me a referral to an oncologist who was an expert in treating pancreatic cancer.

Mistake number one: I didn't really do any due diligence in researching Dr. Lester. I was so scared—*so* scared —that all my brain could handle was to blindly follow any doctor's orders.

I couldn't get an appointment with Dr. Lester for two days so for what seemed like the longest two days of my life, I continued to be an emotional wreck. Scared shitless. Shallow breathing because I was so frightened. I had trouble sleeping, even more than I normally do.

I kept going over the very few details I'd been given. I had a tumor. In my pancreas. No context. I knew nothing about its seriousness or lack thereof. I wasn't even 100 percent sure it was cancer, but my brain was telling me it was death-sentence cancer.

I thought I was going to be dead in three months. I thought I was a dead man walking. For those few days, I cried buckets of tears. The recurring obsessive thought of not seeing my kids grow up tore my heart out. Where would they go to college? What would they major in? What kind of careers would they get into? Who would they marry? Would they have grandkids I would never meet?

Keep in mind that nobody had told me I'd be dead in three months. Nobody had told me anything.

But the panic side of my brain took over. And that wasn't pretty.

Susie drove me to Dr. Lester's office in West Los Angeles, just a few miles from my house. We went into his office and sat down. I was fully expecting the doctor to look at me, bite his lip and say, "There's really nothing we can do."

I should probably mention that the first two things I noticed about Dr. Lester were that he was overweight and out of shape and that he was sipping on a Diet Pepsi. Red flags that I ignored at the time.

If I had to guess, I would say he was in his late 60s, possibly early 70s. He was quiet. Serious. Didn't smile. A man of few words. I learned over the next few months that those were the nicest things I could say about him.

Dr. Lester looked at the scans I'd had the two days before, and then looked at me and said,

"So, what do you want to know?"

In my head, I was like: *What do I want to know? You fucking asshole...I know nothing. Nothing. Am I going to die?*

Of course, what came out of my mouth was different, but I essentially said the above in a much nicer way.

He gazed at me without smiling—without much emotion at all—and with a look that I initially misinterpreted as just social awkwardness and perhaps an odd way of dealing with people, and said, "You're going to be okay."

He then proceeded to explain that he thought it could be one of two types of pancreatic cancer, and that a biopsy would need to be done to confirm which type. He suspected it was third stage adenocarcinoma, which he referred to as a "garden variety cancer."

Garden variety? Maybe to you!

A biopsy was scheduled for the following week.

Dr. Lester said the tumor had been in my body for "many years" (weird to imagine that) and it was slow-growing. It had just gotten to the point where I started to feel its effects.

He said the tumor was in the tail of the pancreas (at that point I had no idea that the pancreas had a tail), had wrapped around a blood vessel and that for now, it would be too dangerous to attempt to surgically remove it or to treat it with radiation.

They would have to shrink it with chemotherapy treatments once a week over the course of six to nine months and then the plan would be to perform surgery.

I had to start chemo immediately. And, soon after the biopsy, I would have a port installed in my chest to make the chemo infusions easier for intake.

It all seemed so overwhelming. I was happy that Susie was with me to hear all of this because I knew I wasn't comprehending everything. I was getting scared again. A biopsy. A surgical procedure to have a port installed. Chemo immediately.

I needed reassurance. "Wait, you told me a few minutes ago that I'd be okay. All of this sounds really scary. Am I going to be okay?"

He said yes again.

So that Wednesday was a much better day. *Much better.* And to be able to tell my boys this news, after the news of two days prior, was lovely.

I wouldn't know that I had actually been misdiagnosed by Dr. Lester until a few months later.

FOUR

The New (Ab)Normal

The day I found out about the tumor in my pancreas, I knew almost immediately that I was in "The New Normal." Life was not going to be the same. Unfortunately, I didn't really know what The New Normal entailed. Whoever was in charge had forgotten to send me the memo.

Really, there's no such thing as The New Normal. I'd been trying to create a sense of "normalcy," but nothing about a cancer journey is normal.

Since I had a tumor in my abdomen, I could have also called it The New (Ab)normal.

For the first few weeks, I felt helpless and powerless. I knew that I was certainly not in complete control, but I thought that at the very least I could help define and shape what The New Normal meant. (That actually may have turned out to be correct.)

After the initial shock of the news wore off, I started becoming much more active: asking for specific help from people (not easy) and asking those who had been through something like this for advice about keeping my mind and body healthy during the months of chemotherapy that were to come.

When musician Sharon Jones died at the age of 60 from complications due to pancreatic cancer in November 2016, just a couple of weeks after I was diagnosed, it freaked me out. I had just seen her perform four months before at the Mammoth Lakes Blues Festival, and in between songs, she had been talking about her bout with cancer. She said her treatment was going well.

So, when she died from the same cancer I had just been diagnosed with, I was really scared and sad. I had to accept that hearing bad news about other people dying of this disease and how it impacted me was part of The New Normal.

Also, as part of The New Normal, I stayed off the internet. I didn't want to go down the "research" rabbit hole. Social media and Google can be your best friend and your worst enemy, sometimes simultaneously.

In addition, I tried to set limits on what I was allowing people to tell me. For example, I tried to limit what people told me about their friends or loved ones dying or suffering from cancer. I was totally open to success stories, however.

Many people who knew what I was going through used the words "your illness" or talked about me being sick.

Clearly, I was in denial at that time. I didn't consider myself to be ill or sick. I just figured that I had this growth in my pancreas that needed to come out. And the doctor had told me I was going to be okay. Part of the refusal to consider that I was sick or ill was that I was continuing to be very physically active. I was hiking, practicing yoga and working out in my chiropractor's pool.

"I'm not sick," I would tell almost everyone.

And I really didn't feel sick.

That said, there certainly were times when I didn't feel

well. I would soon learn that the chemo would kick butt on my stomach. And would make me tired. Plus, I still had the abdominal discomfort that led me to get checked originally in October.

And I certainly felt depressed. And even a bit angry at having to go through this.

Also, I was definitely experiencing stress. And anxiety. And fear.

I wanted to acknowledge to my blog readers that I was relaying only *my* experiences. I understood and realized that others who had been through this kind of thing had had experiences that were similar to mine—or entirely different.

I was attempting to juggle the intense fear, the small amount of denial and a dose of optimism. It was quite the emotional stew.

Chemo made most of my hair fall out. The plus? I didn't need to shave! As for how it was impacting my stomach and my overall well-being, I soon learned that chemotherapy had originated from the mustard gas used in World War II. Don't believe me? Look it up. Knowing what I know now, I'm convinced that in 20 years or less, using chemotherapy to treat cancer will be looked upon as archaic.

As Dr. Mossgale told me, "Chemo isn't a smart bomb." It can kill the bad stuff. Unfortunately, it also kills some good stuff.

Over the next few months, I would learn to dread chemotherapy, and not just for the side effects. In my case, it wasn't even killing the bad stuff.

FIVE

The Pancreatic Tales

As I received the results of my biopsy and started chemo, I wanted to keep my readers updated. By December 2016, this is what I had been told:

- There are different kinds of pancreatic tumors. Mine was called adenocarcinoma.
- It had been in my body for years, growing slowly.
- It was only in the last few months that it grew large enough to where I could feel symptoms.
- The tumor was located predominantly in the "tail" of the pancreas.
- The tumor was not small. It was also not the size of two bowling balls. (I'm not sure where that came from, but roll with me—no pun intended.)
- The tumor was wrapped around a blood vessel, which meant surgery and radiation were too dangerous to be viable options without first shrinking the tumor with chemotherapy.

- The cancer had not spread to other organs and thus was officially classified as stage III.
- The cancer had not spread to my lymph nodes.
- Dr. Lester had called it a "garden variety" tumor. I still kind of half-smile when I hear that because what the fuck does that even mean? Anyway, I would unfortunately learn within three months that he turned out to be amazingly wrong about that characterization.

I re-named the blog "The Pancreatic Tales" after it became clear that the earlier title, "A Good Hair Day," was no longer going to work. I'd been blessed with a good head of hair all my life. Then it fell out. For a few days, it was drip, drip, drip. Then it started coming out in clumps. It was sad, fascinating and just plain strange.

After shedding hair like crazy for seven to 10 days—a constant reminder of what I was going through—I sauntered off to see Andrea, who I call my Hair Don't stylist. She buzzed my head. The good news was I still had hair. It was just really short.

Around this time, I was trying to decide how to tell the blog readers about the depression I had been feeling pre-diagnosis. The depression had been scary-deep. Suicide-thought-provoking-deep. It was so therapeutic to write down my thoughts and feelings, but I was worried about how they would be received. In the end, I decided I wasn't ready to share. Despite my goals of being raw and authentic about my experience, I wasn't able to be fully honest until later.

SIX

Bruce Springsteen and Me

Several years before my diagnosis, one of my professional peers was diagnosed with colon cancer. Aside from his family, and perhaps a few of his employees, no one knew of his condition. Once in a while, I'd hear tidbits about his health from people who presumably knew more than I did. Overall, his health was a closely guarded secret.

I remember thinking that if I was ever going through something like that, I didn't want it to be a secret. I didn't want people wondering or speculating. I would be honest and open about my situation. Not that Sam's way was wrong. It wasn't. It was what worked for him and his family.

Starting in my late 30s, I had decided that I wanted to live a more authentic and honest life. My friend, Jordan Roberts, reminded me of something we'd learned from the therapist we were both seeing at the time, Dennis Palumbo.

"I don't do happy for my clients," he said, "but I do have some experience teaching my clients to have an increased capacity to bear the discomfort they will naturally feel when they finally start to behave authentically."

The desire to be even more authentic became that much more pronounced after I received my cancer diagnosis, though it did come with the cost of discomfort.

About my depression: the summer before my diagnosis, I'd started to feel it deeply. I mean *deep*. Different than sadness. Different than acute depression, which is part of the human experience. Different than I experienced when my dad died in 1986 or when my mom died in 2008.

I was feeling so down, so worthless, so hopeless, so useless and so unnecessary that I started having major suicidal thoughts. In my head, I wrote a suicide note. And rewrote it and rewrote it. I never put anything on paper. But I couldn't shake this horrible feeling. I wanted to get my affairs in order. I wanted out.

I couldn't figure out why. My life was overall going pretty well. I had some things going on with my back (not related to the tumor). I was in great physical shape. Work was going well. I had money stress, but I almost always had money stress. My relationship with Susie was going well. And things were copacetic with my ex-wife, Carmen. We'd had a "good" divorce and were pretty much always on the same page with co-parenting. Stuff with the kids was stuff with the kids, mostly good, but what parent doesn't get humbled every day?

But this depression was so deep and so real. It was really, really scary.

During the summer of 2016, I was on a backpacking trip with my teenage boys. My happy place, in Yosemite. And I was expecting to have a great time.

And sometimes I did. But the waves of depression were rough, particularly on this trip. A couple of times, I had to stop and find a place to be by myself. I'd lie down and breathe just so I could get through the bad feelings. My younger son, AJ, noticed. He asked me a couple of times on that trip, "Are you okay?"

The thought that my kids were noticing something dragged me down even further.

I kept all of this to myself. I was too scared and ashamed to say anything to anybody. And that made it worse.

I thought depression and contemplating suicide were signs of weakness.

I thought I could "power" my way through this.

Finally (and luckily), I knew I had to start talking about it. I had to get out of my own head.

Bruce Springsteen's memoir was published around this time, and he gave a series of interviews about his on-and-off depression years. I remember thinking if one of the biggest rock stars in the world could go public about this, then I could have the courage to open up to people close to me about what was going on.

In early September, I decided to tell both Susie and my therapist, Pamela. Just giving my thoughts an outside voice eased the pain. It eased the depression a bit. I also told Carmen, though I was afraid to tell her how severe it was, because I worried that she wouldn't want me around the kids. I then told a few close friends. Telling people about what was going on was the key. Keeping it inside had been poisonous.

I also started taking supplements to help with my depression and insomnia. Prescription drugs have never been my friend, so I stayed away from those.

And things started getting a bit better. The deep suicidal thoughts eased.

Then, just as the depression seemed to be easing, I started feeling the abdominal symptoms.

I don't understand anatomy, physiology, body chemistry or how the mind works well enough to explain this, but doctors and studies have all confirmed what I'm about to write: the depression was an early symptom of the cancer. It was the first sign that something was going horribly wrong in my body. There is a clear linkage between depression and pancreatic cancer.

To be clear, the depression didn't cause the cancer. The cancer likely caused the depression.

The struggle with depression has since ebbed and flowed. Try getting a deadly cancer diagnosis and see what that does for your mood!

After sharing my truth about my depression with people close to me, I finally went public with it in a blog post. I received more comments on that post than on any other. Most people commented about how courageous it was to talk about this stuff.

As the saying goes, "You might as well go out on a limb, because that's where all the fruit is." Of course, that limb could also break and you could fall on your face.

For the first few weeks after the diagnosis, I could sum up my feelings about cancer in a few sentences:

1. It's scary.
2. It's time-consuming.
3. As one of my friends who had cancer a few years ago wrote to me, "The fear will subside with time, but life will never be the same."

The fear. The doubts. The wondering. If this has been in my body for years, is there something else lurking that could also kill me?

It was a rabbit hole I went down far too often in the first few months. Heck, the first two years.

I was also trying to treasure the gifts that were arriving even though they were tough to see sometimes. The biggest gift was the love that my family, friends and blog readers were giving to me in various forms.

In December 2016, I wrote this in one of my blogs: "My will to live has never been stronger. Never."

That belief would be tested many times in the years after.

In early October 2016, four weeks before my diagnosis, I was fortunate enough to meet Bruce Springsteen and shake his hand at a book signing in Portland, Oregon. In my 15 seconds with him, I thanked him for his bravery and honesty for speaking out about his years of depression. Oh, and I was also able to thank him for the greatest and most moving performance I had ever seen in my lifetime of concert-going, his show at the New Orleans Jazz and Heritage Festival in April 2006, eight months after Hurricane Katrina.

SEVEN

The Rabbit Hole of Fear

Let's be clear. I never loved chemotherapy. For the first month or so, I thought I could handle it, despite my hair falling out. Despite the awful metallic taste in my mouth that never went away. Despite the fact that I knew I was poisoning my body. I figured I just had to get through it.

I was going in once a week for treatment, three weeks on and one week off. It was not a barrel of laughs. Most of the time, I was in a large, charmless room lined with patients in treatment chairs, kind of like a beauty parlor.

It was a morose place to be. There were two TV monitors mounted on the wall, but they were never operating. I had very few conversations with other patients and did not witness many conversations, either. Even though we were all lined up right next to each other, we weren't talking.

I remember one week at the clinic, chatting with the nurse who was hooking up my IV. Wanting to lighten the mood a bit, I said, "Geez, it's like a morgue in here." She didn't laugh.

I had to look for the small things in the midst of what was a pretty miserable period. After a few weeks, the doctor gave me permission to do my pool workout again. And they took off a chemo pump I'd been wearing full-time during some weeks, which allowed me to actually shower like a normal human being.

Susie and I started hiking again in the Santa Monica Mountains. I also got into the pattern of taking long afternoon naps. When I was alone, which was often—I had the kids half the time and I worked from home—I thought too much. I would visit and revisit the dark recesses of the rabbit hole of fear. Sometimes I thought I lived there.

Writing the blog reduced my loneliness and kept my mind active and distracted. Susie suggested that it was also a way to create a support group. My support group. And when I started getting such positive feedback on the blogs, I realized that others were getting something out of my writing as well.

Still, every day, I was scared. What if my chemotherapy doesn't work? Are the doctors not telling me something? Even though I was pretty much pain-free (though not discomfort-free), would things get worse?

One of my long-held beliefs about humanity is that women live longer than men because they are better at showing their emotions. After I was diagnosed with cancer, I cried. A lot. It helped, and so I let the tears roll.

Some still believe that men still aren't supposed to cry, right? Well, I think that's bullshit. Being diagnosed with cancer and undergoing chemotherapy is a good reason for anyone to cry.

EIGHT

Turning 60

On December 19, 2016, less than two months after my diagnosis, I turned 60.

Cue the balloons from the rafters! The celebratory music! The gifts! The parties!

Or not. I was having severe side effects from the chemo instead.

Back when I'd been blissfully unaware of this thing growing inside my body, I was ambling toward 60 with a mild sense of dread. It sounded so *old*. How had life flown by so damn quickly?

After my Halloween Day Surprise, I went through the first few chemo treatments thinking, "Well, this isn't fun, but this isn't a disaster."

A couple of days after my last chemo infusion, a few days before my 60th birthday, I started having some very uncomfortable stomach issues. (You don't want the gory details, trust me.) In addition, my throat got really sore, and my lips were very burned. My skin itched like crazy. I had that ever-present metallic-poison taste in my mouth. I was super fatigued. Exhausted, actually. And scared. Always scared.

This went on over my birthday weekend, when Susie and I were in Laguna Beach, trying to have a good time at the Ritz-Carlton.

It was so not fun.

My one-sentence summary of a "How I spent my 60th birthday" essay would be: I spent it in bed sleeping or in the bathroom.

I tried to force myself to adopt a Zen-like "It is what it is" attitude.

Which sounded good, in theory.

I would get there *maybe* 10 percent of the time. The rest of the time, I was so not Zen.

In addition to the fear and the physical symptoms, I was starting to feel both sad and angry, sometimes simultaneously. I was ashamed when I looked at my body in the mirror. I felt like it had violated me. I felt like my body might be dying. It was unbearable to see.

I tried to remember that life throws you curveballs once in a while. Or to continue with the baseball metaphor, sometimes the batter gets beaned by the ball. But unless the batter gets knocked out (very rare), he has to get up and get back in the batter's box and face the next pitch.

So that's what I tried to do. Get up and dig into the batter's box and wait for the pitcher to throw whatever he was going to throw.

In December 2016, I initiated the Chemmy Awards to be given out periodically to the person who had written the funniest, the most meaningful or the most memorable comment on my blog.

Yes, "Chemmy" is the marriage of "chemo" and "Emmy."

The comment below was a text from a friend named

Barbara with a very dark sense of humor. Her comment was in response to my blog about depression and suicide.

"My oh my, you are hitting the top 10, aren't you? Well, this is all good and brave, but the real test to me comes when you describe the size of your penis."

Ahem.

Rest assured I did not and won't be writing about that.

And I hope you appreciate the humor in this as much as I did.

Obviously, Barbara won the first "Chemmy" for the most inappropriate yet hilarious comment in response to a blog post.

Around the time of my birthday, I crowned a second Chemmy Award winner, but I didn't think it was appropriate to print the actual quote.

Now I do.

The Chemmy winner was Jordan Roberts of Venice, California. He's a dear friend, a lovely human and a wonderful and funny movie director and screenwriter.

"You are a beautiful man. Seriously. Love your self-acceptance and the great care you grant yourself. You're trusting your instincts and that's deeply moving. You might be as close to a truly evolved, soulful and heart-centered man I know, if only you didn't fuck those two sheep."

This was the best birthday present I could have ever received.

NINE

MTHRF

As part of the original blood work that I had done three days before my diagnosis back in October, Dr. Mossgale tested me for the MTHFR gene mutation.

No, sorry to tell you that MTHFR does not stand for motherfu****. It stands for methylenetetrahydrofolate reductase. It's a genetic defect (we all have them).

Rather than trying to explain it fully (because I can't), I'll refer you to the Wellness Mama blog where it's discussed in detail. The short version is I have a genetic mutation that makes it hard for me to process folic acid and B vitamins...which can lead to many different health problems.

My interpretation, based on limited research and conversations with doctors, is that the study of MTHFR is in its infancy stage. It seems like much more is unknown than known about this genetic defect, and what (if any) illnesses it can lead to. Again, this is just my interpretation. I'm not a scientist.

The blood test results showed that I tested positive for this gene mutation. And one of the possible ramifications of having this gene mutation was that it may have made it more difficult for my body to flush out toxins.

At least that's what Dr. Mossgale was suggesting to me.

He wasn't saying, "This is what happened and this is why you have the tumor."

But he was saying that it was possible.

What I didn't know at the time was that it might have also been why I was having so much trouble with chemo, and why it wasn't working (which I didn't find out for three more months). Chemo is toxic. And if the body has trouble getting rid of the poisons, bad things can happen.

Much of this information was making my head swirl. It was confusing because there was no apparent consensus in the scientific community about MTHFR. To avoid the swirl, I realized that I needed to focus more on what to do about my cancer rather than fixate on *why* I had gotten cancer.

TEN

Christmas 2016

The cumulative effects of weekly chemotherapy treatments had been kicking my butt for the two weeks prior to Christmas.

The chemo made me tired, which contributed to my sadness and depression and fear. Mentally and physically, I was compromised. I couldn't think clearly and I couldn't be as active as I wanted to be.

Since the separation from Carmen in 2011, the Christmas morning tradition was for us and our two sons to do a gift exchange at her house in Santa Monica.

I was so not in a good emotional or physical place when I arrived at Carmen's house that morning.

After quick hugs and short pleasantries with my boys, gift unwrapping began. My boys were 14 and 12 at the time. So even though Christmas was no longer about Santa, the holiday still had significant meaning, if only because it was a chance to celebrate as a family unit—and exchange gifts.

I watched my kids open their presents quickly and with their usual glee.

But, as was often the case during this phase of my cancer experience, my mind started to drift and then descended into the rabbit hole.

My thoughts started like this:

I love my kids. It's so nice to be here.

And quickly descended to:

What if this is the last Christmas I will be alive to celebrate with them?

And then I was drowning:

This will definitely be the last Christmas I will be alive to celebrate with them.

The voices in my head were so far removed from the reality of that morning. I was forgetting to breathe and starting to panic. And I was hiding all of this. At least I was trying to. I don't think my kids or my ex-wife knew anything about what I was feeling or thinking.

I excused myself to go to the bathroom.

In the bathroom, kneeling on the floor, I started to cry and then completely lost it and started to uncontrollably weep. Heaving, deep crying, to where I couldn't even begin to try to stop myself.

I had convinced myself that I was going to die sometime before next year's Christmas festivities and that my kids were going to grow up without their dad. I wouldn't get to see them as adults. I wouldn't get to see them in their careers. Wouldn't get to see them with spouses. Wouldn't get to see them with their own children.

I wouldn't even live long enough to watch them graduate from high school.

Christmas morning of 2016 was the absolute worst.

ELEVEN

"I Didn't Get It"

My head was not in a good place. I was fearing imminent death, my body felt like shit, my confidence was shot and the thoughts of missing out on seeing my kids grow up were ever-present. I would imagine not seeing Susie's beautiful smile or laughing with her anymore and it would bring me to my knees in tears.

In late December, I finally texted my oncologist to express my concerns, and his quick response was, "Try not to worry."

That's it. Not "How are you?" Not "I know this is tough." Not "Give me a call" or "Come into my office."

Try not to worry.

I decided he had no idea what I was going through. I was starting to deeply resent this man.

I found much more hope in a blog post sent to me by Vicki Stolberg, a friend who'd survived cancer. The post had been published by an oncology nurse earlier that year. Nurse Lindsay had been diagnosed with third stage colorectal cancer in September 2016, just a month before I received my diagnosis.

What Nurse Lindsay expressed was more powerful than anything I could write to that point, and it moved me to tears.

Dear Every Cancer Patient I Ever Took Care Of, I'm Sorry. I Didn't Get It.

This thought has been weighing heavy on my heart since my diagnosis. I've worked in oncology nearly my entire adult life. I started rooming and scheduling patients, then worked as a nursing assistant through school, and finally as a nurse in both the inpatient and outpatient settings. I prided myself in connecting with my patients and helping them manage their cancer and everything that comes with it. I really thought I got it. I really thought I knew what it felt like to go through this journey. I didn't.

I didn't get what it felt like to actually hear the words. I've been in on countless diagnoses conversations and even had to give the news myself on plenty of occasions, but being the person the doctor is talking about is surreal. You were trying to listen to the details and pay attention, but really you just wanted to keep a straight face for as long as it took to maybe ask one appropriate question and get the heck out of there fast. You probably went home and broke down under the weight of what you had just been told. You probably sat in silence and disbelief for hours until you had to go pretend everything was fine at work or wherever because you didn't have any details yet and wanted to keep it private still. You probably didn't even know where to start and your mind went straight to very dark places. That day was the worst. I'm sorry. I didn't get it.

I didn't get how hard the waiting is. It's literally the worst part. The diagnosis process takes forever. The different consults, the biopsies, the exams and procedures...and the scans. Ugh, the scans. You were going through the motions trying to stay positive, but at that point, you had no idea what you were dealing with and the unknown was terrifying. Knowing the cancer is there and knowing you're not doing anything to treat it yet is an awful, helpless feeling. I'm sorry. I didn't get it.

I didn't get how awkward it was to tell other people the news. You didn't know what to say. They didn't know what to say. No one knew what to say, but there was some relief when the word started to spread. It may have been overwhelming to reply to all the calls and messages—and to get used to others knowing such personal information, but this nasty secret you'd been keeping was finally out and your support system was growing. I'm sorry. I didn't get it.

I didn't get how much you hung on to every word I said to you. You replayed it in your mind a hundred times. Did I really mean this or that…you wondered if you understood. You called me again to make sure. And maybe another time because your friend asked, "Well, what about _____." You asked your other nurses to see if you got the same answer. Please know we are happy to take a million calls a day with the same questions until you can make sense of it. I'm sorry. I didn't get it.

I didn't get how much you Googled. I told you not to do it. You did it, a lot—and so did I. Searching for information, hope, stories like yours, reassurance. It was impossible not to. My new stance is to just know what a good source is when you Google. I'll help you learn to filter the information. And I promise to give you more information, because I know how much you crave it. It's not realistic to think you will have the willpower to not search at all (at least it wasn't for me). I'm sorry. I didn't get it.

I didn't get what it felt like to get the sad looks all the time. Walking down the hall at work or seeing someone for the first time after finding out. You got the head tilt with a soft "How aaaare you?" You quickly got together your rehearsed "Doing pretty good, tired but hanging in there" generic response. Don't get me wrong, I know you appreciated all the well wishes and concern, but it sure took a little while to get used to the pity. I'm sorry. I didn't get it.

I didn't get what really goes on at all those "other

appointments." I knew what to tell you to expect at your oncology appointments, but all the different types of scans, radiation, operating room, procedural areas—I didn't really know what went on behind the scenes there and what to tell you. I should've known more about the whole picture. I should've been able to warn you that there was an hour wait after a dose of medication before you could actually have a scan. I should've been able to tell you what you can and can't eat or drink before a certain procedure or that some treatments require going every single day. I'm sorry. I didn't get it.

I didn't get how weird it felt to be called "brave." It's a word that gets thrown around a lot, yeah it kind of made you feel good, but you still didn't really understand why people would call you this. Sure you were getting through it fine (most days), but it's not like you had a choice. I'm getting treatment because I have to. It doesn't really make me feel like much of a hero. I'm sorry. I didn't get it.

I didn't get how crazy this makes you. Like you literally wondered if you had lost every working brain cell. Especially when dealing with side effects or other symptoms. You could've had every side effect in the book from chemo or none at all and you'd still wonder if it's really working the way it's supposed to. You may just have had a headache, or a common cold, or a sore joint, but you were never certain it wasn't related to your cancer and always wondered if it was a sign of progression, even when it made no sense. I hope you didn't feel dismissed when you called me to ask about it and I said not to worry. I'm sorry. I didn't get it.

I didn't get why you were always suspicious. You couldn't help but wonder if they all knew something you didn't about your prognosis. We shared the percentages and stats with you and told you that every cancer is different, but still, is there something more? Something they were protecting you from or just felt too bad to tell you? Logically, I know the answer to this but find myself with these feelings as well. I'm sorry. I didn't get it.

I didn't get how confusing "options" really were. In some cases, there may be more than one choice. Whether it was physicians, medications or sequence of treatment, I would try my best to help you understand every angle, but more options many times just meant more confusion. You wanted to be involved in your own care, but the stress of too many options was sometimes too much. You begged me for my input and to tell you what I would do if it were me. I hated that question, but I hear you now. I'm sorry. I didn't get it.

I didn't get how hard it is to accept help. Especially the moms. This just wasn't something you're used to doing, but you needed it. You felt shy about admitting that you weren't sure you could've gotten through the first few months without the extra food, gift cards, support and other help you were given. You felt humbled at the outpouring and just only hoped you would've done the same for them. You still wonder if you said thank you enough or if you missed an opportunity to give back. I'm sorry. I didn't get it.

I didn't get the mood swings. One day you felt confident that you'd completely beat this with no problem; you felt like you could take over the world. And for no good reason, the next day you were just as convinced yours was going to be one of those sad stories people tell their friends about. The moods snuck up on you without warning. Literally anything could've been a trigger. I'm sorry. I didn't get it.

I didn't get that when you said you were tired, you really meant so much more. Sure, there are words like exhaustion and extreme fatigue, but there should really be a separate word just for cancer patients, because it's crippling. Really. Some days you really wondered how you'd trudge forward. I'm sorry. I didn't get it.

I didn't get how much time this really takes away from your life. I always used phrases like "Cancer is like getting another full-time job" or "Life doesn't stop for cancer" when trying to prep you for what you were about to embark on. But now they just seem like corny catch phrases. It completely took over, you had to stop doing things you love, you had to cancel plans, you had to miss out on things that were important to you. It just wasn't in any plans—and that alone took a lot of mourning. I'm sorry. I didn't get it.

I didn't get how strange it was to see your body changing so quickly. You stood there and looked at yourself in disbelief in the mirror. Maybe it was extreme swelling, maybe it was scars, maybe it was hair loss, maybe it was pounds melting away when you do everything in your power to eat as much as you can. It's hard. Your appearance is tied more closely to your identity than you'd like to admit, and these were constant reminders of what you were up against. You just wanted to feel like yourself. I'm sorry. I didn't get it.

I didn't get that it hurts to be left out. People didn't invite you to things anymore. People felt like they can't complain or vent about everyday annoyances to you anymore. People acted differently towards you and it hurt a bit. You certainly didn't blame them— you had even done the same to others when traumatic life events happened—and no you didn't want to go out for drinks anyway because you don't feel good. But you needed normalcy. I'm sorry. I didn't get it.

I didn't get how much you worried about your kids. For this, I'm the most regretful. I should've talked to you more about them— and not just in terms of lifting restrictions or germs. You worried about how this was going to affect them. You worried about not being able to keep up with them or care for them properly on your bad days. You worried they'd be scared and confused. You worried about leaving them. I'm sorry. I didn't get it.

I didn't get the guilt you felt. Especially to those who are married. You thought about how unfair it was that your spouse had to pick up so much slack—mentally to help keep you focused and calm, and physically at home pulling double weight with never-ending everyday chores. You understood that everyone promises "in sickness and in health" when you get married, but you still felt like they didn't deserve this. You felt thankful when your spouse would say, "Go get some rest and I'll take care of the kids," but your heart hurt overhearing them play in the other room away from you, wondering if that was a glimpse into their future that didn't have you in it. I'm sorry. I didn't get it.

I didn't get that it never ends. Never. I used to tell you that cancer would be just a phase in your life. Just like high school or something. It seems like it drags on and on when you're in it, but soon it'll all be a memory. I'm sorry if this made you feel marginalized — it is not a phase. Yes, there are phases. The treatment won't last forever, but you are changed now. The worrying won't stop, the uncertainty won't stop, the fear of recurrence or an awful end won't stop. I hear that gets better. Time will tell. And time is precious. I'm sorry. I didn't get it.

I do have to admit; I've probably had it a little easier than you to start off. I know the language, I know all the right people, I work where I get treatment so sure, it's more convenient. I watched so many of you march through this terrible nightmare with a brave face and determination—without knowing one thing about cancer ahead of time, other than knowing you didn't ever want to get it. You've always been my inspiration and I love each and every one of you. Nothing brings me more joy than when I see you reach your goals and slowly put yourself back together. I love when we get visits or notes from those of you who are several years out and doing great. It's good for the oncology nurses' soul. Even though healthcare workers don't really know what it's like to be you (well, us) it's ok. Nobody does. I just hope that I was still able to give you a little guidance and strength to help you get through your cancer treatment. Even if I didn't get it.

Love,
Lindsay, Oncology RN

TWELVE

The Pity Look

Nurse Lindsay's words hit me on so many levels. I felt like I had finally found someone who one thousand percent understood what I was going through.

One passage in particular stood out:

I didn't get what it felt like to get the sad looks all the time. Walking down the hall at work or seeing someone for the first time after finding out. You got the head tilt with a soft "How aaaare you?"

I called it The Pity Look. And I had definitely gotten it many times. Too many times to count.

It was very difficult to get used to. I was struggling at times with my own emotional pain, which made it challenging to see the pain in the faces of others. Sometimes I would avoid social encounters because I didn't want to get The Pity Look.

I knew that The Pity Look was a person's expression of love and good intent. But I also thought, *Are people afraid of me? Am I contagious? Radioactive?*

I lived with the difficulty of being on the receiving end of The Pity Look for a long time.

THIRTEEN

Making Cancer Fun

I was scheduled to get a CT scan at the end of January 2017. But in early January, I told my oncologist, Dr. Lester, that I was feeling the discomfort of the tumor more than I had in the past and it was scaring me.

It was such a weird feeling to describe. I never had pain, but I definitely thought I was feeling the tumor. Unless I was wrong? Was it the side effects of the chemo? Was it all in my head?

Dr. Lester decided to schedule a scan immediately instead of waiting a few more weeks, mainly to put my mind at ease but also to see if the chemo had shrunk the tumor.

I went to UCLA Medical in Westwood for the scan. If you haven't been there, the UCLA Medical buildings look like a mini-industrial complex. It's gigantic and very intimidating.

A few days after the scan, I received very disappointing news: Dr. Lester told me that the tumor had actually grown a tiny bit. Not much. But it was obviously not what he wanted. Nor what I wanted to hear.

The chemo had not been working.

While I was trying to process this news, Dr. Lester told me we were onto Plan B. He seemed surprised that Plan A had failed.

I was slowly losing confidence in him.

Plan B was to run a special blood test that day. It would take one to two weeks to get the results and was a very specialized and expensive test that my insurance would not cover. But it was supposedly going to drill down to the DNA level to reveal what chemical treatments would work in the place of the first round of chemo.

I was lucky that I could afford to do this. What about the people who didn't have the money? Why was our health insurance system so screwed up? And why didn't Dr. Lester tell me about this test back in November?

It was then that I was reminded of the "Standard of Care," a health insurance term that is widely used in the medical industry—and, yes, it's an industry.

Here's a real-world example of "Standard of Care": Back in 2012, after I'd had some routine blood work done by my regular doctor, Dr. Mossgale, all the results came back negative except for a slightly elevated cholesterol number. Dr. Mossgale referred me to a cardiologist, who promptly ran a battery of tests.

I passed all of those tests except for one. The cardiologist prescribed statins, a commonly used pharmaceutical for elevated cholesterol levels, and insisted that I start on them immediately.

I went back to see Dr. Mossgale. He slowly pored over the test results, sat silently for what seemed like a long minute and then said to me, "Chris, you don't need statins. At least not now. Get in better shape, work on your diet and eat healthier. Then we will re-test you in a few months."

Happy (because I hate taking drugs, prescription or recreational), I asked Dr. Mossgale why the cardiologist had prescribed the drug and why she had never discussed diet or exercise with me. His response? "Prescribing statins is the 'Standard of Care' dictated by the insurance companies. If the cardiologist didn't prescribe this and you had a heart attack, she could be sued. And perhaps lose her medical license."

I was like, *What the fuck?*

This is but one example of how screwy our medical system is here in the United States.

Anyway. Back to cancer.

Standing up to leave Dr. Lester's office on the day I received the bad news about the chemo not working, I asked him, "Will I be okay?"

He confidently replied, "Yes." His confidence had not wavered.

I would love to tell you that mine had not wavered, but of course it had.

I had a big cry in the car on the way home, and so did Susie. It was the first time I saw her in tears about my cancer. She had mostly kept her fear and sadness from me.

I told Susie, "I feel like I've fucking wasted the last two months of my life!"

Susie tried to make me feel better by making me laugh. She had some suggestions for how to spiff up Dr. Lester's very drab, gray and depressing offices. Perhaps a disco ball could hang from the ceiling in the room where the patients were receiving their infusions?

Amidst the laughter and the tears, we coined a new motto. "Making cancer fun."

FOURTEEN

Thinking the Worst

I was worried about my health, stressed out about the worrying and stressed about being stressed.

It was vicious. Every morning in the shower, I would fall to my knees and break down in tears.

The day we coined Making Cancer Fun, I posted a link to a clip of George Costanza from *Seinfeld* getting a phone call that he thought was a cancer diagnosis.

I have almost always thought the worst when I'm anticipating some personal news. For example, every test I took in college—every test—I would walk out of the classroom thinking I had flunked. Was it true? A couple of times, yes, but mostly I got A's and B's. But in the time between taking the test and getting the results, I was in misery. I would torture myself.

After my father died of cancer in 1986, I found a small lump on my back and was petrified for an entire year. It took me a year just to go to the doctor because I was convincing myself that I would be dead within months. The lump turned out to be a benign cyst.

I'm that person. I often think the worst.

So, when I got a diagnosis that was worthy of scaring the crap out of me, it wasn't good. My brain went to thoughts of death very fast and returned to those thoughts frequently. In my head, everything all sort of blended together, a toxic stew of negative thoughts.

For me, dealing with the fear and the emotional fallout from the cancer diagnosis was a huge challenge during the first three months. It was second only to the side effects from the chemotherapy treatments.

Then we started on Plan B. The side effects of the new chemotherapy regimen were much worse: severe nausea, diarrhea, vomiting, skin itching like crazy and intense fatigue. For the first few weeks, I stopped writing and exercising. I was just sleeping a lot during the day.

I was starting to wonder if I could take care of myself, let alone still be an active parent to my kids. Susie and I even interviewed home nurses who would be paid to stay with me most of the time to help take care of me.

My depression returned with a vengeance. I wasn't sure how much longer I could endure the toxic stew of chemotherapy and its side effects, as well as the fear and depression. I started checking my life insurance policies to see if my loved ones would be covered if I decided to end my life.

Several people reached out to me asking if my lack of writing meant I wasn't doing well. That was partially true. But I didn't really disclose that to too many people. The physical effects of the chemo were kicking my ass, but uncertainty was kicking my ass harder. I had no way of knowing if Plan B was working or not.

I continued to struggle with my emotions and fears. It became much more debilitating than any of the physical effects of the cancer or the chemo. I got angrier, I wallowed in self-pity, I thought way too much.

One night in February 2017, I attended my first pancreatic cancer support group meeting at a cancer center in West Los Angeles. I'd been hesitant to go, mainly because I'd had enough sadness and fear in my life and didn't want to be around others who could make me feel even worse.

My instincts were correct. I listened to very sad stories of cancer journeys that didn't end well. Perhaps if my emotions had been in a better place, I could have been more receptive. As it was, I had no desire to be there and I never returned.

I started putting limits and boundaries on my in-person and phone conversations with people.

I would tell many some version of the following:

I don't want to talk any more about this right now, and please don't take it personally. I love and very much appreciate your concern, the outpouring of affection, the wondering how I'm doing. But I'm tired of hearing my own voice and I'm tired of talking about cancer.

It was much more interesting for me to hear how others were doing. Or to talk about sports. Or politics. Or the Grammys.

Or anything but cancer.

FIFTEEN

One Step Up, Two Steps Back

During a mid-February 2017 visit, Dr. Lester put a bottle of OxyContin in his hand to show Susie and me. There were probably eight to 10 pills in the bottle.

I held my breath because I had no idea what this man of few words (and, seemingly, few emotions) was about to say.

I held my breath because the opioid epidemic had killed about half a million people in the United States over the last 20 years.

I held my breath because I hated taking pharmaceutical drugs.

I held my breath because I wasn't really in any serious pain. I had discomfort, yes, but my bigger problem was that the chemo had been kicking my ass, not the cancer.

"I don't want to take pain pills," I said before Dr. Lester had a chance to speak. "I'm afraid of getting addicted. And I'm just having a little pain, nothing major."

Dr. Lester looked at me with contempt. With daggers in his eyes. This was a man who, I had learned over the last few months, didn't like to be questioned and didn't tolerate dissenting opinions. About anything. Whenever Susie or I would question him, his face would scrunch up with disdain. I could tell he was pissed. And offended that I would even dare to question him.

"Did you know that they've done research on monkeys and these pain pills are safe for monkeys and monkeys do fine with them? Are you smarter than those monkeys?"

I was speechless. As was Susie.

"Look, you can take this entire bottle of pills all at once and it's not going to hurt you."

If my jaw could have dropped to the floor, it would have dropped to the floor.

Later, I would wish I had replied, "Maybe you should take all of those at once and let's see how you do?"

I wound up taking maybe three pain pills over the next few days. I hated them because they caused constipation and made me groggy. When I texted Dr. Lester about the side effects of the pain pills, he predictably prescribed some drugs to ease the constipation.

These discussions with Dr. Lester got me to a breaking point. I didn't want more pain pills or medication to ease constipation. Enough was enough.

The next two weeks were particularly rocky. I had to keep going back to Dr. Lester's office to get IVs for nausea, anxiety and dehydration. The combination of the physical and emotional side effects of the chemo and the cancer had weakened me horribly. I was getting more depressed. And anxious. Panicky. And I still didn't know if Plan B was working or not.

Things were so bad that one night in early March, I had Susie take me to the emergency room at UCLA. I thought I wasn't coming out of that hospital alive. I really did. I was calling and texting my company's office manager, Andrea, on my way to the hospital to make sure my paperwork was in order so that my kids, Susie, her son and Carmen would be okay financially.

As it turned out, I wasn't done. I was terribly dehydrated and anxious and after receiving a few IVs and getting some sleep, I was on my way home.

That night, I knew something needed to change.

The following morning, I was scheduled to receive a chemotherapy infusion from Dr. Lester.

I canceled the appointment.

Over the course of the next few days, I debated whether or not I should stop chemo altogether. I wrote about it in a blog:

I'm not 100 percent certain of this yet, but I am strongly considering trying a different approach. I have started doing research into cancer treatment centers outside of the US, because much of what is practiced in other countries is not allowed here. I have opinions on that as well, and I'm guessing those of you who read my Facebook posts know what they are. But let me say this: People like me need different options here in the United States.

And, as my friend of a friend Bobby Tessel said to me (Bobby was successfully treated at one of these centers in Germany in 2016 for his bladder cancer and as of this writing is cancer free): "I don't consider what I did alternative treatment, it's just alternative to the United States."

I can't pinpoint with 100 percent certainty why my struggle seems so difficult. But in a general sense, I have never thought my body was built for massive doses of Western medicine pharmaceuticals. Growing up with a mom who was a nurse and also a prescription pill popper, I really never had confidence in it even as a kid. My mom died eight years ago, and one of the things I feel contributed to her death and her mental illness over many years was the massive amounts of prescription drugs she put into her body during her lifetime.

Can I prove any of this? I cannot. I am giving my opinion, my experience and my intuition.

I am not against Western medicine. Some of it is an absolute miracle. But we are all built differently. Some people can't eat peanuts. Some people can't drink red wine without breaking out. I have never felt that Western medicine and I were a good match.

So, I will keep you posted as to what I decide. I'm not going to agonize over the decision. And I'm well aware that whatever I do that I certainly could die.

There are no guarantees.

But I just feel like at this point I don't want to die of side effects of the chemo and taking pain pills. And that's what I've I felt like. I've been on a path to death not caused by the cancer itself.

I am asking for this even if you don't agree with me: Your understanding. Your continued love. Your continued support. And your respect.

I didn't know it yet, but when I called to cancel that appointment with Dr. Lester, it would be the last communication I would ever have with him.

Within a matter of weeks, I would learn how mistaken Dr. Lester had been about my entire treatment plan and how wrong he had been about the cancer itself.

The Next Few Months

SIXTEEN

The Goodbye Letter

Thinking I might not be around much longer, I composed a letter to my boys:

Dear Jasper and AJ:

I write this letter to you in early March 2017, not knowing what the future will bring.

The truth is, we rarely really know with 100 percent certainty what the future will bring.

It pains me deeply to not be able to spend as much time with you both as I have in the past.

Dealing with this illness, as you know, has been very challenging.

Please know that I hope in the near future we can start enjoying more time together, and resume going on our travel adventures and enjoying life!

In the meantime. I want you to know some things.

First, I love you so, so much. More than I can write. More than I can ever say. Love like I've never experienced before, Jasper and AJ. I never experienced unconditional love until I had children.

Getting to help raise you and watch you grow into great young people you have become is the greatest gift ever. EVER.

You boys are such wonderful kids. Keep doing what you are doing.

Study and work hard in school. Lots of people are smart. But not everybody works hard. That's a difference maker.

Listen to people. Really listen. Remember that when a person is talking, they aren't listening. We learn more from listening to others than we do hearing ourselves talk.

Be fearless with love. It took me a long, long time to learn this one. Don't be afraid of love. Move towards it. Embrace it. Lean into it. Own it. Cherish it. And most importantly, once you find it, work hard at it. Really hard.

Give. Remember that not everyone is as fortunate as we are. Find ways to give to others. To be of service to others. The organizations that I was a part of creating—the ones helping the musicians in New Orleans (which you know I stumbled into sort of accidentally and organically)—changed lives. Including mine!

Embrace life. We never know how long we will have.

It's ok to have fears. Everyone has them. What I've learned is to figure out how to walk through the fears. I've seen you both do this already in so many different ways.

It's ok to cry. Don't ever let anyone tell you that it's not ok for boys or men to cry. It absolutely is.

Not everyone is going to be nice to you all the time. Including your parents. :) Remember that we are all dealing with our own emotions, our own fears and our own insecurities.

Communication will help. Try to talk (or write) to people if you're hurt or feel you have been wronged. Don't focus on what they have done. Focus on how you are feeling.

Be genuine with apologies, and own and learn from your mistakes.

Drink lots of water every day! Stay hydrated! It took me decades to learn this.

Eat healthy. Eat moderately. Eat consciously.

Exercise. Get outdoors every day. Every day. Being outside feeds the soul.

Hike. Bike ride. Swim. Travel.

Be kind to people.

Not everyone will be nice to you all the time. But be conscious that if someone is not being nice to you, it says something about them. Not about you.

You have so many opportunities in front of you. Live them to the fullest.

I love you both so much.

Dad

I never sent this letter to them.

SEVENTEEN

Crappaccinos

A few days after the short visit to UCLA Emergency, I made the decision to end treatment with chemotherapy. Some might now consider that to be bold. At the time, I had no idea if it was courageous or just plain stupid.

I had no Plan C at that point. When I quit, it was with the very primal thought that Plan A didn't work and Plan B was killing me. I was either going to die soon or hopefully find something else to treat the cancer. I felt alone, naked, scared and surprisingly liberated.

I made an appointment with Dr. Melanie Gisler in West Los Angeles, who I had known for many years. I made the decision to see her not only because I had always liked and respected her, but also because I didn't want to see Dr. Mossgale, who had recommended Dr. Lester.

Under Dr. Gisler's care, I embarked on a new treatment plan in late March of 2017 that included:

1. High-dose vitamin C drips
2. Glutathione drips

3. Large doses of vitamin supplements and enzymes
4. Mistletoe injections
5. Coffee enemas (Pamela, my therapist, called them "Crappacinos")

I could spend pages talking about these various therapies. I won't, as that's not the intention of this book. But I will tell you this: my body started to feel better, almost immediately. Admittedly, that could have been mostly because I was no longer doing the chemo. I will never know. Oh, one thing to mention: coffee enemas can be pretty messy.

In addition to seeing Dr. Gisler, I sought out many different nutritionists, who gave me very conflicting advice. *You need to keep meat in your diet! Grass-fed only beef! No, do not eat any meat! No dairy! Don't drink alcohol! Watch your sugar intake! Go on a keto diet! No, keto isn't good for pancreatic cancer! No caffeine!*

The only thing that seemed consistent was that everyone said to stay away from processed sugar, so I did just that. I lowered my sugar intake. And I became much more conscious of what I was putting into my body. I read food labels in a more serious way than ever before. And I read a book by Michael Pollan called *Food Rules*. It offered a common-sense approach to choosing healthy foods and became a sort of mini-bible for me.

I decided I needed to figure out what the best nutrition program was for *me*. I became convinced that this wasn't a "one size fits all" situation. I needed to eat healthier and in a way that fit my lifestyle. It was a lifestyle that did not include cooking.

One thing I kept in my diet: oysters.

I refer to Susie as my partner in brine. Yes, you read

that correctly. Together, we've developed a deep love of raw oysters. We've learned about their origins, their geographies and their flavor profiles. Around this time, we started writing about our oyster escapades on a Facebook page called What the Shuck?

See? Susie and I were making cancer fun.

EIGHTEEN

It Takes a Village

When I was a kid, my mom taught me a bunch of stuff related to health and medical care, mostly based on her experience as a registered nurse.

The main lesson she taught me was this: Be your own doctor. Always ask questions. Make your doctors and nurses sit with you. Get them to listen to you and to spend time with you. Doctors can often be linear thinkers. Get second opinions. And make your own decisions based on what you think is right or wrong for your situation.

It was great advice that I didn't follow at the beginning of my cancer journey. I was so petrified and so paralyzed by my fear and all I wanted was for a doctor—any doctor —to save my life.

I didn't question Dr. Lester much and I didn't get a second opinion. Instead, I blindly took his advice.

Doctors aren't gods. They are trained in their area of expertise and not necessarily the areas beyond it. For example, I was surprised to learn that most medical doctors don't receive any more than a few days of training in nutrition.

I had put my oncologist on a pedestal and blindly followed him and it almost cost me my life.

As I searched for whatever Plan C was going to be, I started doing research on doctors and clinics who didn't follow the traditional "Standard of Care" path for cancer treatment, which included radiation, chemotherapy, surgery or some combination thereof. I found various "alternative" cancer centers in Mexico, Santa Barbara, New York and Germany.

Years before my diagnosis, I had heard about Dr. Nicholas Gonzalez in New York City from my friend, Michael O., who had been diagnosed with prostate cancer in the 1990s. I knew that Michael, under the care of Dr. Gonzalez, had taken hundreds of supplements (enzymes, vitamins and minerals) a day and that it had helped.

During my research period, I found that Dr. Gonzalez had authored several books discussing what he called The Gonzalez Protocol. He'd also written a paper called "Four Reasons Why Cancer Patients Routinely Die."

In this paper, Dr. Gonzalez writes that patients routinely die because they make these four mistakes: they panic, they are unable to make decisions, they believe in the myth of authority and they believe in the myth of credentials.

Wow. I had already made the first mistake and was dancing with the third and fourth mistakes. I had panicked. I had thrown myself under the care of authority figures without doing any of my own research. I started to realize how close I had come to being one of those "cancer patients that routinely die."

Dr. Gonzalez, unfortunately, had died of a sudden heart attack in 2015. His business partner, Dr. Linda Isaacs, was still practicing in New York, so I called her office and asked how I could get treated.

I was instructed to follow their online protocol for prospective new patients, which included sending medical records and writing a detailed letter discussing my condition and how I had been treated to date.

I sent my materials to Dr. Isaacs on March 27, hopeful that I would be accepted and fly to New York for treatment.

Unfortunately, that's not what happened. A few days later, I got a call from Dr. Issacs' associate, who said, "Dr. Isaacs doesn't take new patients who have been previously treated with chemotherapy." Apparently, she felt that it could compromise her work. If a patient wasn't responding to chemo, she thought The Gonzalez Protocol might fail because the recipient was too weak or too far gone.

Admittedly, I took this as rejection. Dusting myself off, I moved on to other possibilities.

Bobby Tessel was diagnosed with bladder cancer in January 2016. A mutual friend of ours told me about Bobby's story. He wasn't happy with the Western medicine approach offered to him in the United States (his doctors wanted to remove his bladder and prostate), so he decided to head to a German cancer clinic called Infusio for alternative treatment. After spending four weeks at the clinic in Frankfurt, he was told he was cancer-free about a month after his return and remains so at the time of this writing.

I contacted Bobby and he told me "the reason I went to Germany for treatment is because the cancer treatments they do there are not approved in the States. I do not consider what I'm doing to be 'alternative medicine.' I just consider it alternative to the United States."

Between talking to Bobby and doing online research, I learned that Infusio offered tons of treatment options Dr. Lester and I had never discussed—because he didn't offer them: stem cell therapy, hyperthermia, daily IVs containing high-dose vitamin C, ozone therapy, Myers cocktails and more.

While different from a traditional United States approach to treating cancer, it was complementary to the treatment I had started under Dr. Gisler.

The cost, including treatment, a place to stay, airfare and food was going to be about $50,000. And my medical insurance was not going to cover a single penny. I scrambled to figure out how I was going to come up with this money.

I was so, so lucky. A good friend and fellow school parent, Julie Glassman, who knew about my plight, created a GoFundMe page to help raise the cash.

With my blessing, here's what Julie posted on GoFundMe on March 30, 2017:

Our friend Chris Joseph is not your average guy. Nope. He's funny as hell. Sharp as a tack. And deeply loving and connected, despite his insistence that he's anything but.

He's also a dedicated and impassioned father (of two). A (loving) ex-husband (of two). The (unbelievably lucky) boyfriend of (one) remarkable woman—and the step-boyfriend-dad (ish) to her (one) seriously adorable son.

He also happens to have cancer. An icky one. Pancreatic. One that's taken his heart, mind and spirit in many directions. Some full of resolve and determination. Others rife with fear and dread.

A cancer with odds that are daunting.

A formidable opponent…

And a total mf-ing drag.

After going the traditional chemo route to beat this thing, Chris's body retaliated and resisted. His cancer neither retreating nor relenting—instead growing and asking: "Is that all you got?"

Never one to settle, and always the adventurer, Chris responded with a big idea. A big risk. And an even bigger f-u to cancer: If I can't beat this with traditional, FDA-approved strategies and techniques (he thought), I'll go overseas where more progressive treatments are available…and more importantly…working. Shortly thereafter, stronger than ever in his resolve, Chris found a cancer treatment program in Frankfurt, Germany. One that's working. One that's employing alternative techniques, technologies and methods to kick some serious cancer ass.

His plan is to be there starting April 21, for about 23 days— to take a chance on dendritic stem cell therapy and daily IVs containing different things from immunomodulation to anticancerogenic. He'll also undergo Hyperthermia to "cook" the cancer cells, Thymus injections, Ozone-Treatments and Cranio-Sacral therapy. So much good stuff, it's almost like a spa—but not at all.

Which brings us here. These German treatments aren't cheap…even with the Euro. And, as you can imagine, medical insurance covers NONE of it (no Obamacare or repeal jokes please).

So his many friends, who've been sitting by (impatiently) waiting for him to ask for help (which he never does), came up with the idea to start a fundraising campaign to pay for travel, treatment, his stay and incidentals (bratwurst, beer, etc.)

We need $50,000—and fast.

So please open your hearts, open your minds, open your wallets. Help in any way you can. Every penny counts—and April 21 is just around the corner.

Thank you in advance and much, much love.

-Chris's Peeps (all of whom need him around to make them laugh [and cringe] for many years to come)

https://www.gofundme.com/lets-help-chris-kick-cancers-ass

Within two weeks, 318 people had contributed to the

fundraising effort, with a cumulative total of just over $63,000.

I was stunned. Shocked. Humbled. And, so, so grateful to have a village of people willing and wanting to help me on the next phase of my journey.

The trip to Germany was a go.

But before I departed, there were still some obstacles to overcome, shocking things to learn and blessings to create.

NINETEEN

It Takes a Village, Again

Since the late 1980s, I had attended the New Orleans Jazz and Heritage Festival every year except for one. Jazz Fest, as it is commonly known, showcases all manner of music styles, including rock, rap, hip-hop, R&B, folk, zydeco, Cajun, pop, country and jazz. So if you were to say, "Oh, you must really like jazz," I would gouge my eyes out. It's not just jazz!

By attending every year, I made dozens and dozens of friends. I "met" many of these friends on the Jazz Fest online chat board before I met them in person. We became known as the "Threadheads" because of, you know, "chat thread."

In 2005, the Threadheads organized a "backyard" music party in New Orleans between the two weekends of Jazz Fest. Inspired by a misspelling of "party" on the chat board, the gathering became known as "The Patry."

In August, months after the festival, New Orleans was utterly devastated when the levee system failed during Hurricane Katrina. About 80 percent of the city was underwater, hundreds of thousands of homes were lost or damaged, thousands were killed or injured and many more thousands were displaced to other areas of the United States.

The Threadheads knew and loved many of the musicians who had lost their homes and wanted to do something—anything—to help their plight. So in 2006, the backyard music Patry became a fundraiser. The proceeds went to the New Orleans Musicians' Clinic, a non-profit that provides medical services to performing artists in the city.

As Jazz Fest approached in 2007, many of our musician friends in New Orleans were still suffering. That year, Paul Sanchez and John Boutté, two well-known New Orleans musicians, played the opening performance at the Patry as a duo. It was magical. During the set, in their banter and story-telling between songs, John asked if Paul would produce his next record.

After the set ended, I wandered up to John and Paul and asked, "When would the two of you put out a CD together?"

Paul's succinct response, with his sly smile, was something like, "Well, that would take money. And many of us still don't have permanent housing. We are still struggling to even pay rent."

From that conversation, an idea was born. Over the next few weeks, I decided to raise money from the Patry attendees for both John and Paul to make their own solo albums, with the stipulation that the musicians would pay back the Threadheads from the sales of their records.

Their CDs, John Boutté's "Good Neighbor" and Paul Sanchez's "Exit to Mystery Street," were released several months later. Within a few months, both Paul and John paid back the money the Threadheads had donated.

That created an opportunity for the next idea. If we

could do this for Paul and John, could we do it for other musicians in New Orleans?

This was how Threadhead Records was born. Using the "borrow and pay back" funding model, about 60 records were made by dozens of New Orleans musicians over the next few years. Hundreds of musicians were employed by the musicians making the records.

Local and national press, including newspapers, magazines and radio and television news stations, covered the story and amplified what the Threadheads were doing.

It was crowd-funding well before crowd-funding was a term. And, as far as those of us involved knew, it was the only fan-funded, volunteer-run record company in the world. It was a record company that never sought to profit and that purposely didn't own any of the publishing rights or master recordings to the music. It was done solely out of the love for New Orleans, its music and its musicians.

The Threadhead Records motto was "Rebuilding New Orleans, One Song at a Time."

In 2009, I helped start a separate organization, the non-profit Threadhead Cultural Foundation. Its goal was to promote the cultural heritage of New Orleans through grants and assistance to musicians, artists and others involved in endeavors relating to music and other artistic expressions. The work of all these artists is in the tradition of preserving, promoting and disseminating the cultural heritage of New Orleans and the surrounding areas of Louisiana. Since 2009, the TCF has handed out nearly three-quarters of a million dollars in grants and performance money.

The mark that the Threadheads made on New Orleans was and continues to be significant. The musicians and their families and friends were so grateful and thanked us often.

Musicians often said to me, "This organization changed my life." Whenever I heard this, I was reminded of the scene in the 2009 movie *The Blind Side* when Sandra Bullock's character, Leigh Anne Touhy, is talking to a friend about the impact of her taking in a homeless teen:

Friend: I think what you are doing is so great. Opening up your home to him…honey, you are changing that boy's life.
Leigh Anne Touhy: No. He's changing mine.

That's how I felt. We had changed their lives and they had changed ours.

In February 2017, Paul, who had by then become a close friend, was working on his latest album. During February and March, we were texting about that, my health situation and his difficult divorce proceedings. We were both going through life-altering events.

I wrote, *I hope this river of tears turns into tears of healing.*

Paul loved that line. Within hours, he'd written a song with that title and given me a co-writing credit.

In subsequent texts, I wrote that Paul's wife was "long gone." Boom. Paul wrote another song and gave me another co-writing credit.

The day before Paul was to finish recording the album, then tentatively titled "Tears of Healing," we were texting again.

Me: *What a ride this is.*
Paul: *Life is quite a ride.*
Me: *Song for the next album?*
Paul: *Don't get me started or it will be in this one.*
Me: *Let's do it.*

Within minutes of having that text exchange with Paul, I wrote this:

It starts with a first breath, and then with a cry.
It ends with a last breath, on the day one dies.
And in between life is a ride.

I sent this to Paul, and immediately after I hit "send," I cringed. My inner voice said, *Paul is going to laugh. He's going to hate this.* I felt shame that I would even dare to suggest lyrics to an award-winning songwriter.

Paul loved what I had sent. He said he was going to write some music to the lyrics, and while he was off doing that, more lyrics came out of me that I sent to him:

It's confusing, mysterious and sometimes not fair.
And most of the time we're not in charge of what's here or what's there.
And in between life is a ride.

Double boom. Paul worked with famed New Orleans songwriter Alex McMurray to finish the song with some additional lyrics, Paul wrote the music, and the song was completed. And it became the title song of Paul's album, "Life is a Ride."

Music writer and fellow Threadhead Steve Hochman, who helped raise money to produce the album, wrote these liner notes for the CD:

When Paul Sanchez turned his, and his city's, unfathomable challenges in the week of the 2005 flood into art, Chris Joseph gave him the vehicle, creating—spontaneously and organically—the fan founded not-for-profit Threadhead Records. That, in turn, took on its own life in subsequent years, with hundreds of fans supporting dozens of artists and a much-needed stream of musical light shining out of New Orleans darkness. Now as Chris has faced his own life challenges, Paul has helped give him a vehicle of expression, helped draw out inner most feelings into words, into poetry—and into song. It's mutual inspiration at its best and most profound, extending to the whole community of musicians who stepped in and the family of Threadheads and beyond who stepped up to support this album, all done with love, grown from the seed Chris planted back then. That's the Ride of Life.

-Steve Hochman, pop music journalist, Los Angeles Times

What a ride I was on.

TWENTY

Warrior Pose

A couple of years before my diagnosis, I devoured a book called *Warrior Pose: How Yoga (Literally) Saved My Life* by Brad Willis. A former NBC News war correspondent, Willis had been diagnosed with stage IV throat cancer in 1998 and had also suffered a broken back and a failed surgery. Given no more than two years to live after radiation and surgery for his cancer, he turned to the ancient practices of yoga, which include fasting and physical purifications along with yoga postures, breath work and positive thinking. He has currently been cancer-free for more than 20 years.

After I moved on from Dr. Lester, I remembered Brad's book and started reading it again.

As coincidence would have it, the brother of a good friend heard about my health situation and (without knowing I'd already read the book) reached out to me to ask if I wanted to be introduced to Brad Willis.

Of course I did!

In mid-March, I started working with Brad online. He shared his wisdom about yoga, meditation and nutrition. Our talks were also very inspirational. Brad had done what

I wanted to do: figure out a way to navigate my health care on my own.

The weekly chats with Brad lifted my spirits. After a few months, I drove down to his house in Coronado for a day-long visit and we dove deeper into yoga and meditation, took a bike ride on the beach and enjoyed a very healthy lunch.

One of Brad's suggestions was to continue blogging, but to vlog instead of just writing. So I did just that, starting with two Facebook Live video blogs a couple of days before leaving for Germany.

Brad and I talked a lot about fear. He sent me an article he had written, which included this passage:

> *What I mean by survivor fear is that every time I get a sore throat or catch a cold, a little voice in the back of my mind says, "Maybe it's back." It sends chills down my spine every time.*
>
> *I used to fight that voice with everything I had. The funny thing is that my resistance made it even stronger, like a scream. All my meditation, relaxation, guided visualizations and other self-help tools didn't help at all. I felt something was wrong with me. I was a coward. A hypochondriac. Wallowing in self-pity. Going crazy. Or maybe it really was back and I had better plan for the end. It drove me crazy.*
>
> *What's taken me years to realize is that this is normal. Extremely normal. I can't imagine any cancer survivor not hearing this voice now and then, even though we all handle it differently. What I have found that works for me is to accept it. Even "hug" it. Yes, wrap my emotional arms around that voice and give it a hug. "You again. I don't blame you for whispering this. It makes sense to me. Thank you. I appreciate you. I know you have my best interests in mind and are just trying to help." Once I accept it, thank it and hug it, it dissipates much faster without all the dark scenarios I used to conjure up.*

Modern mind/body science has proven the deep connection between our emotions and our inner chemistry. Fear empowers the body for an emergency, but at the same time it drains energy from the immune system. Calmness boosts our immune system. In my own healing journey, it was calmness that, along with a vegetarian diet, yoga postures and meditation, facilitated my healing. I still practice every morning. Of course, I get agitated and anxious about life sometimes, but there is always a pathway back to calmness, acceptance and gratitude…especially now that I can hug that voice of fear.

Brad Willis was an early and integral part of my healing journey, and I am in deep gratitude to him.

TWENTY-ONE

The Misdiagnosis

After I fired Dr. Lester in March 2017, I typed his name into Yelp and found a few very negative reviews. Please note that I'm definitely not recommending that anyone make a choice about medical providers from reading reviews on Yelp. That said, it can be a useful tool to gather information.

An excerpt from 2011:

This is the most INsensative (sic) doctor with whom I have had dealings. He is cold and compassionless. Why didn't we change doctors? That's a question I keep asking myself.

From 2013:

He is heartless. Despite dealing with individuals in critical physical states he lacks empathy and compassion. He does not explain treatment regimens and is bothered when questions are asked. When my relative was having significant difficulties, I called his office three times on one day requesting a call back as I sought Dr. Lester's direction regarding need for urgent medical care. I never received a call back and sought emergency care. Despite the fact that he had been her treating doctor for over six months he NEVER had the decency or humanity to call and learn of her status. Regretfully she died a few days later.

From 2019:

Dr. Lester has to be analyzed in two different ways: as a doctor and as a person. As a doctor, he arguably has the most effective way of treating pancreatic cancer. His method did not work for my mom who passed away within a few months of starting treatment with him, other doctors disagree with his methods, and his study showing his success has holes in it, but there is evidence that his method is better than others.

As a person, Dr. Lester is scum of the Earth human trash. When I came to ask him questions to determine whether we should use him for my mom's cancer, he told me that I had to ask him questions only and that I could not set up the questions with facts before asking the questions (what?), he made fun of me and my questions, he told me that I was rude for texting on my phone while my sister was asking him questions and he would not let it go even after I put my phone away, he would not respond to my emails, he would not do a genetic test for us even though he told my sister on many occasions that he would, he told my sister that he would suture her mouth closed if she asked him to do a particular operation on my mom again (she had only asked once before), etc. Mind you, this is all while we are in an extremely vulnerable and fragile state dealing with my mom's cancer.

Lesson learned from Dr. Lester: I would never blindly put my health in someone else's hands again.

Dr. Gisler, a general practitioner, was everything Dr. Lester wasn't. Curious. Responsive. A great listener. Warm. Friendly. Caring. Asked a lot of questions. Talked about food and diet and nutrition. Talked about exercise. Spent time with me. And here's the biggest thing: she asked oncologists she trusted what they would recommend for my situation.

One afternoon in late March of 2017, Dr. Gisler asked me if I would give my approval to have a sample of the biopsy I had done that past November sent to a lab called Caris.

I didn't think twice about it. Dr. Gisler thought it would be good to do some genetic testing of the tumor. Without having any idea of what the results might show, or of the implications of those results, I was onboard. What did I have to lose?

A few days before I left for Germany, the results came back from the lab. I had a rare genetic condition called microsatellite instability (MSI), which can cause mismatch repair deficiency (MMR). Ironically, this condition could have been what caused my cancer and was also potentially a key to my future treatment program.

Contrary to what Dr. Lester had told me, the Caris lab results showed that I did not have a "garden variety" pancreatic cancer.

In fact, I had a rare genetic defect that only one out of 100 pancreatic cancer patients have. This condition meant that traditional methods like chemotherapy would not be effective for me.

I had been misdiagnosed!

I was furious. I had wasted four months under Dr. Lester's care. This explained why chemotherapy had not helped my cancer one bit.

Getting misdiagnosed was horrible, but the different diagnosis came with new options.

Johns Hopkins University was looking for patients with my rare genetic condition to take part in a two-year immunotherapy clinical trial, and I was a perfect candidate.

Johns Hopkins invited me to join their clinical trial, which was also being offered at Stanford University, closer to me. For two years, I'd fly to Stanford twice a month for a visit that would include blood work and the infusion of Keytruda.

"This is exciting," I said to the person from Johns Hopkins on the phone, "but I'm leaving for Germany tomorrow."

They told me to call them when I got back. I agreed and started packing.

TWENTY-TWO

Departure

I like to arrive early to all events. Being late is a shameful act in my mind and I avoid it at all costs. Even the thought of arriving right on time makes me anxious. I'm happy to spend two or three hours at the airport before a flight. I'm also happy to start packing a suitcase a few weeks in advance of an upcoming trip.

This is what I did before Germany. I packed everything up and double-checked my passport.

It wasn't set to expire for another three months. I was all set to go.

Ten days before my trip, I was in a session with my acupuncturist, Eugene, who said, "Have you checked your passport expiration date?"

Yep. Three months to go before expiration.

"Some countries won't let you in if your passport expires that soon," he said.

I thought he was joking.

He wasn't.

I either needed to get my passport renewed or Germany would not let me in. And getting a new passport could take at least three weeks, maybe longer. I thought I was fucked. This was so not what I needed a few days before leaving on a trip that I hoped would save my life.

Then I found a private passport service in Santa Monica where I could get a new passport within three to four days.

Bullet dodged.

* * *

Before I left for Germany, I was flooded with mixed emotions. Here's the blog post I wrote on the day of my departure:

I cannot stop crying right now, and while I'm generally willing to share my emotions and thoughts, right now I wouldn't be able to speak on a video.

I just went to say goodbye to my boys. I was biting my lip pretty much the whole time, but started crying as I was leaving. Then I got in the car and the floodgates opened.

They aren't closed yet.

When one has something like this—I don't care how strong a person is, how much he or she breathes or meditates—doubts creep in. Fears creep in. They often co-exist with positive thoughts. But sometimes the fears can be louder.

My biggest fear of the last few months is not necessarily dying, but what can set me to crying in a heartbeat is wondering if I will get to see my kids as adults.

I know there are no guarantees of anything. For any of us.

This life is a gift. My kids have always been an even bigger gift for me. I cannot put into words how much I love them.

When I was saying goodbye to them this morning, the doubts and fears kicked in—will I see them again?

It's time to try and breathe again.

Thanks for reading.
Off to the airport in a few hours.
Love, Chris
#lifeisaride

With the extra money from the GoFundMe effort, I was able to help pay airfare for a few people to join me on the trip so I would be alone as little as possible.

Kurt Oheim, a Threadhead from Amarillo (originally from New Orleans), flew into LAX the day before and accompanied me to Frankfurt. Like many Threadhead friendships, Kurt and I had gotten to know each other over the years in New Orleans. He and I had developed a tradition on the Monday between Jazz Fest weekends. We'd have breakfast at Lil' Dizzy's Café followed by the annual Jazz Fest-sponsored gospel concert at a church in the Ninth Ward. After that, it was po-boys at Domilise's in Uptown New Orleans.

Kurt and I are very different. He's from the South. I'm from Los Angeles. He's relatively conservative politically. I'm not. He's the lead pastor at a deeply Christian-based church in Amarillo. Religion couldn't be less important to me.

But in addition to our shared love of New Orleans, what attracted me to Kurt was that he is one of the nicest, kindest and most giving humans I've ever met. Oh, he also has a pretty good sense of humor.

Kurt was my first of several guardian angels on the Germany trip. He would stay with me for the first five days of the 22-day trip.

TWENTY-THREE

Germany, Part 1

We were greeted at the Frankfurt airport by Angela, Infusio's concierge and coordinator. She could not have been more gracious. We stopped for lunch, and then she took us to our spacious two-bedroom apartment in Frankfurt.

The location of the apartment was great, smack-dab in a walking neighborhood with countless restaurants, shops and parks nearby, including an organic grocery store right across the street. There were kids everywhere. It was a neighborhood that was very much alive, which was exactly what I needed.

During the day and a half before starting treatment, I vlogged a couple of times. One of the blessings from the written and video blogs was that I would get the most amazing feedback. I was so grateful to get the love and prayers that were being sent my way. My heart was overflowing.

But being jetlagged and tired was an open invitation for the doubts to creep in and, sure enough, they did. Why was I here? Would these treatments work? Would I be dead soon?

I also felt excitement, anticipation and hope. I wanted to get started with the treatment program. I felt like a kid waiting for Santa to arrive on Christmas Eve.

Monday at 8:15 am, I was picked up at my apartment by Infusio's driver. We arrived at a newish high-rise building about 15 minutes later and proceeded to the Infusio Clinic on the 15th floor.

The main treatment room had about 10 patient "stations" and contained wall-to-wall windows overlooking a tremendous view of the city and the Main River. It was a stark contrast to the morgue-ish landscape of my former oncologist's office in Los Angeles.

My Infusio doctor, Dr. Bijan Boustani, greeted me with a warm smile and a hug. Bijan (as he wanted me to call him) politely and thoroughly explained my treatment plan for that day and gave me a general outline of what to expect over the next three weeks. On most weekdays, my outpatient treatment would go from about 9 am to 1 or 2 pm. The daily weekday routine was going to be essentially the same, with the exception of the stem cell days (more about that later).

The first day's treatment included IVs of high-dose vitamin C, thymus, glutathione and ozone. My blood was combined with the ozone treatment, then reinjected back into my body. After about 90 minutes of the various injections, I was led to a private room for about 45 minutes where I was to lie down on my back on a hyperthermia machine. The last treatments of the day were craniosacral therapy, reflexology and a glutathione shot in my rear end.

On the first Tuesday after my treatment, Dr. Boustani unexpectedly suggested that I get a CT scan and an MRI. He wanted to make sure that the tumor hadn't grown or spread since the previous scan in January. His request took me by surprise, and by now you should know that I don't like surprises.

On Wednesday, my Infusio driver took me to University Hospital in Frankfurt and dropped me off. I walked into a large hospital in an unfamiliar town. In a foreign country. Kurt had left for the States earlier that morning. I was alone. And scared.

Soon after I checked in, I discovered that my cell phone wasn't getting any reception. None. Zip. I couldn't text. Couldn't email. Couldn't call anyone. And because of the language barrier, I couldn't really talk to anyone at the hospital. I also hadn't brought any reading material because I'd planned to read on my phone.

I was there for six hours. It felt like the longest six hours of my life. When I was finally called in to see the doctor, he looked through the scans right in front of me, which meant that neither one of us knew the results yet. The difference was that my life was on the line. He was just the messenger.

The results were very good. Nothing had grown. Nothing had spread. The tumor was essentially the same size as it was in January.

I walked out of the hospital and started crying tears of relief and tears of fear. Sometimes it was hard to take in even the good news.

TWENTY-FOUR

Germany, Part 2

After Kurt left, Mike Elster arrived. Mike and I have been very close friends since the age of 12. We've watched each other grow up (or pretend to), get married and have kids.

Two stories about Mike:

At his bar mitzvah back in 1970, Mike's parents accused me of switching the signs on the two punch bowls (one marked "Adults Only" and the other not) so the underage kids could drink alcohol. I was never proven guilty in a court of law. If there are any other questions, I will refer you to my attorneys.

The second story is about Mike's mom, Annette, who passed away in June 2019 at 87 years old. She started smoking cigarettes at 16 and continued for 60 years, smoking two packs a day. Mike thinks she smoked roughly 1,000,000 cigarettes in her lifetime.

Annette was an inspiration to me. In her 50's, she started walking about seven miles a day (weather permitting). She never got lung cancer and was pretty healthy well into her 80s.

She was a freak of nature.

I thought of Annette many times throughout my cancer journey. She was a person who did things her own way, moved her body almost every day and managed to live to the ripe old age of 87. She charted her own path and that's exactly what I was determined to do with my cancer situation.

* * *

In Frankfurt, Mike and I laughed a lot. We talked about everything from sports to Donald Trump to our families to our jobs. We took a beautiful walk along the Main River and visited the Städel Museum of Art. It was Mike's first trip to Europe and his sole purpose was to be there for me. That's a close friend.

My first week of treatment ended Friday, two days before Mike left. Dr. Boustani told me his goal was for me to be cancer-free in three months. While I loved hearing that, in hindsight I wished I would have asked him what "cancer-free" meant. I've learned since that there isn't a universal definition of that.

I was glad to have friends with me in Frankfurt, but I was really missing Jasper and AJ. I could text and call them, but it wasn't the same as having them in the same room with me. I sometimes felt that their lives were going on without me. I didn't want to miss anything.

And I really missed laughing with Susie. Susie and I are great at banter. It was hard to do that on phone calls, particularly because I don't enjoy the phone. I never told Susie this, but the truth was that the illness had brought forth insecurities about our relationship. I feared that Susie would get tired of dealing with my health issues and find someone else. I would often look at her and think that she was getting more beautiful every day (which was true), I was dying and she would move on.

I also couldn't go to the New Orleans Jazz and Heritage Festival for the first time in 27 years. It broke my heart not to be there. I missed the music, the food and the essence of Jazz Fest. But most of all, I missed my Thread-head friends.

Fortunately, I was able to listen online to some live music sets on WWOZ, a community radio station in New Orleans. Also, many friends, like fellow Los Angeles Rams fan Mark Rabago, posted videos online. When Paul Sanchez opened his set by dedicating the song "Life is a Ride" to me, I cried.

After Mike left, I was alone, lost in my thoughts and sometimes drifting into the fear cesspool. For decades, I had enjoyed alone time. But now that I had this disease, it wasn't fun. I needed people in my life. I needed connection. Thankfully, my brothers would be arriving soon.

TWENTY-FIVE

If It's Tuesday, This Must Be A Treatment Day

Except that it wasn't a treatment day.

On Tuesday morning, my Infusio driver and I took a three-hour trip from Frankfurt to a very small town in Germany called Bad Harzburg, not far from the old East German border. Bad Harzburg is the home of the small-as-a-house lab facility where I would start the dendritic stem cell process.

I wish Susie was writing an explanation of the dendritic stem cell process because she's much better at facts and research than I am. Early on in our relationship, I told her I was going gluten-free and Susie said, "Do you even know what gluten is?"

Since Susie is not co-authoring this book, I will quote Infusio:

> *"Dendritic cells are found in the bloodstream and are responsible for identifying threats which the body's immune system needs to respond to. When cancer develops in the body, dendritic cells work as antigen presenters for the immune system, ultimately making cancer visible for the killer cells. These immune cells then attack the cancer*

and cause cancer cells to die off. By concentrating your body's dendritic cells, sensitizing them to your specific cancer, and then reintroducing those cells into your system, the 'trained' cells can boost your body's capacity to work against the cancer."

We arrived in Bad Harzburg around 10:30 am and were greeted by Dr. Katrin Pesic, the director of the stem cell and glandular medicine clinic. Dr. Pesic took a few minutes to show me around the facilities and then I was brought to a patient table to sit so she could draw my blood.

More, according to Infusio:

"Monocyte cells are filtered out and exposed to specific growth factors to turn into dendritic cells. The dendritic cells are then 'primed' by being exposed to specific cancer antigens. After seven days in the laboratory, the trained and concentrated dendritic cells will be administered back to the patient through a simple injection or infusion."

I sat for as long as the blood draw took and I was done. I would return to the Bad Harzburg clinic in another week for the stem cells to be reinjected back into my body.

TWENTY-SIX

My Brothers

My brothers didn't know much about the treatment I was doing in Frankfurt, yet they showed up in Germany with their love and concern. They knew I was fighting for my life.

Jeff is three years older than me. We are very different people. Jeff is an indoor person; I'm not. Jeff often does not seem particularly comfortable around people; I'm very choosy about who I spend time with, but mostly enjoy interacting with other humans. I'm into sports; Jeff is not.

Andy is actually a half-brother, 13 years older than me. In certain ways, we have a lot in common: we find the comedy in everything and enjoy banter. In other ways, we have less in common: Andy is a moderate Republican and I'm on the liberal side.

Jeff arrived first, followed by Andy later in the week. On the one night they overlapped, we went to an Italian restaurant near my apartment and they peppered me with questions. *How are you feeling? What treatments are you doing? What is the doctor saying? What treatment will you do when you return home?*

Nights were not my best friend. I was fatigued, which led to a diminished desire to participate in intelligent conversation. I just wanted to be back at my apartment and go to bed.

As we were finishing dinner, Jeff looked at me, burst into tears and said, "I don't want you to die!"

I was speechless. It had never occurred to me until that moment how scared Jeff was for me. He'd lost his wife, Lauren, to cancer a few years before my diagnosis, and our dad to cancer in 1986, so he'd seen the worst.

After Jeff left for the United States, Andy and I had a lovely weekend together. We embarked on a walking tour. We went to museums. We took a tourist boat ride on the Main, where I sampled my first German beer in Frankfurt. I felt like I was finally starting to relax.

But when Andy left, I went back to the feeling of missing. I was missing my kids and I was missing Susie.

I'd always been the more emotional one in our relationship. I cried more easily than Susie did, and over the years she had taken to affectionately calling me Diaper Baby. I had plenty of Diaper Baby moments in Germany. The tears were flowing. I was scared.

I would often remember what my friends who had survived cancer had told me: the fear never goes away. It ebbs. It flows. But it's never gone. A person without cancer eats a meal and experiences the sensation of being full.

Every time I ate a meal, I thought the cancer was growing in my abdomen.

TWENTY-SEVEN

Apricot Pits

While attending high school in the early 1970s, one of my favorite teachers was a professor named Barry Shapiro. Mr. Shapiro was not only a teacher, but also one of my first mentors—a person who really ignited my interest in the environment. One weekend in 1972, we rode our bicycles from the San Fernando Valley to downtown Los Angeles and participated in an "ecology day" demonstration in front of the Convention Center. Mr. Shapiro was a free thinker who wasn't afraid to teach non-conformist material. Being an environmentalist back in the early 1970s certainly wasn't the norm.

Mr. Shapiro also taught us about alternative cancer treatments. One was called Laetrile, which came from apricot pits. I remember pointing to the apricot tree in our backyard around 1972 and proudly educating my parents about it. They thought I was nuts.

Sadly, Mr. Shapiro passed away from cancer a few years ago, but his wisdom followed me to Germany. At Infusio, one of the IV drips I received was Laetrile.

* * *

I returned to Bad Harzburg to receive my dendritic stem cells. This time I was joined by Richard, a very nice gentleman from New York City who I'd met at Infusio the week before.

Richard had fourth stage colon cancer. Nothing had worked for him—not surgery, radiation or chemotherapy. Western medicine had failed Richard; he wasn't doing well.

After our appointments at the small clinic in Bad Harzburg—my "cooked" blood was reinjected into my system; and Richard, who was just starting the process, got his blood drawn—we headed back to Frankfurt. On the drive, Richard told me about what it meant to be a Jehovah's Witness.

He wasn't afraid of death, he said. In fact, a part of him welcomed it. After about an hour, he handed me a small informational booklet from his daypack. Yes, Richard was pitching me on becoming a Jehovah's Witness. I politely declined.

Three months later, Richard passed away from cancer. It was a stark reminder that there were no guarantees when it came to treatment. Maybe apricot pits helped. Maybe God helped. It was impossible to know what was helping and what was not.

TWENTY-EIGHT

The Rest of the Last Week in Frankfurt

In Frankfurt, I finally decided to start meditating. Even though I had practiced yoga for more than 20 years, I'd never been able to do a deep dive into meditation.

My friend and former business partner, Jim Brock, recommended an iPhone app called Headspace. With it, I practiced twice a day for about 20 minutes total. Did it help? I have no idea, but I knew that becoming more conscious of my thoughts could only be a good thing.

I had also been given a mantra by my friend, Brad Willis. "I am healing. I am healing. I am healing." Simple and straightforward. I tried to repeat that as much as possible.

After Andy left, my friend and acupuncturist, Eugene Iwasa, arrived. Eugene was on the second leg of his six-week European vacation and had agreed to stay with me for a few days during the last week of my treatment. Eugene spent the days sightseeing while I went to treatment, and then we'd have dinner together. It was wonderful to be in his comforting presence.

On Thursday of that last week, I randomly got a text

from my friend, Jeff Gutheim, who was visiting Frankfurt with his sister. Jeff, Eugene and I had dinner together, and I tried schnitzel for the first time. Jeff is one of the funniest people I've ever known; laughing our asses off at that dinner was one of the highlights of my trip.

On Friday, my last day of treatment, I received the usual assortment of vitamin drips, another hypothermia treatment, 30 minutes of reflexology and then Dr. Boustani set me up with various supplements and materials for IV drips to take back to Los Angeles.

He also gave me some sage advice about my diet. Like everyone else, he advised minimizing my sugar intake. "But," he added, "one has to enjoy life." Once in a while, it was okay to have a dessert or a glass of wine. In other words, we don't have to be perfect.

That Friday night, I had a very nice conversation with Susie's brother, Ed Delava, who had rerouted his business trip in Israel to accompany me home to the United States. The following morning, we went to the airport together, where Ed surprised me by upgrading my ticket to first class. It was such a generous gesture, one of so many I had encountered over the last several months.

On the flight home, I felt so much gratitude and love for the friends and family who'd stayed with me during my three weeks in Germany; for those who helped fund my trip; for the Infusio clinicians who treated me like royalty; for a very understanding and loving girlfriend who supported me one thousand percent; and last but certainly not least, for my boys, who had taught me more about resiliency than anyone else in my entire life.

I remembered how when Jasper was seven years old, he broke his femur skiing at Mammoth Mountain. Three nights in the hospital over Christmas 2009, two surgeries, a walker, physical therapy and four months later, he was almost back to normal. I remember asking him what he had learned from his ordeal. His response? "I could get through it."

It had been almost seven months since my cancer diagnosis, almost two months since I had quit chemotherapy without a plan and only a few weeks since I had decided to embark on an alternative path.

I was getting through it.

After Germany

TWENTY-NINE

Coming Home

When I landed at LAX, I saw that Susie had tagged me in a Facebook post that said, *My man is coming home today* accompanied by a heart emoji.

What Susie has taught me over the years is that love is a verb. I also learned over the years that when Susie gives an expression of love, she one thousand percent means it.

After getting through customs, Ed and I walked to the baggage area where Susie was waiting to greet us. It was so wonderful to see her, to hug her, to hold her and to kiss her. Three weeks was a long time to be apart, especially under the circumstances.

About 30 minutes later, Susie and I pulled into my driveway in Santa Monica. I walked into a house that had been decorated with a large *Welcome Back, Dad* sign, balloons and streamers.

Later, Carmen dropped Jasper and AJ off at the house. To see the boys smile in person and to exchange hugs was amazing.

It was great to be home.

But as I fell asleep in my own bed that night, some of

the doubts and fears kicked in again. *I'm going to die soon. None of what I'm doing has worked. I'm going to let down all those friends who supported me on my trip to Germany.*

The more rational part of my brain knew that I felt a lot better than I had two months earlier. I was now certain that I would no longer exclusively look to Western medicine to treat me.

Still, I had no idea if any of the alternative treatments that I'd started in Los Angeles and continued in Frankfurt were working. No cancer treatment is guaranteed.

I calmed myself down, tried to stay positive and reminded myself of the plan. I would continue to be active in determining my treatment. I would be my own CEO, as my therapist, Pamela, liked to put it. In the meantime, I had support. I would be resuming treatment with Dr. Gisler soon.

THIRTY

Why Did I Get Cancer?

I've been asked this question often. The short answer is, I don't know.

The longer answer is that I have various theories. Keep in mind that some or all of these could be true—or not.

1. Family history? My dad died at the age of 77 of lung cancer. He had been a smoker for about 30 years and lived in smog-filled Los Angeles for about 50 years. My dad's siblings had died from cancer, though not pancreatic. Other than them, I'm not aware of anyone in my immediate or extended family who had cancer.

2. Smog? I lived in the San Fernando Valley for most of the first half of my life. For those of us who grew up in that area in the 1960s, the air pollution was really bad. I remember how after playing at recess for 30 minutes my lungs would be wheezing for about two hours. Think about the cumulative effect of breathing that type of air for decades.

3. Side effects from recurrent staph infections? For about eight years, starting when I was 16, I got staph infections in various places on my body: face, arms, legs, fingers, back. I took medication for the infections. Were there side effects from those infections or from the treatment?

4. Gut issues? I've had at least three bad stomach infections over the years: salmonella from food I ate in Mexico in my early 20s, giardia (a few times) from untreated water in the Sierras in my 30s and campylobacter from brushing my teeth with unfiltered water in Nepal in my mid-40s. Could cancer have resulted from that?

5. Leached mercury fillings? Some dentists and doctors have postulated that mercury fillings can slowly leach into the body, causing very bad side effects. As we know, mercury is poisonous. I had my mercury fillings removed two years ago after a few experts had advised me to do so.

6. Vaccines? Now, before you get agitated even reading that word, know that I'm not anti-vaccine. That said, I've done a ton of research on vaccines since my kids were born. Some are much more effective than others. Some have side effects for a small percentage of people. And some doctors and health practitioners think too many vaccines in too short of a time period can have potentially bad side effects. At any rate, the reason I bring this up is that Carmen and I had our bodies bombarded with various vaccines before our honeymoon in Nepal and Thailand in October 2001. Side note: the "travel doctor" from whom we

received these vaccines no longer practices as a travel doctor.

7. My unique genetics? I've been diagnosed with MTHFR, which makes it difficult to flush out toxins, as well as MSI, which can cause MMR. Could any of these conditions have caused my cancer?

8. Drugs my mom took when she was pregnant with me? My mom was a notorious prescription pill popper. Did she ever take thalidomide, the sedative discovered in the 1950s that was prescribed to pregnant women to relieve anxiety and morning sickness? Later, thalidomide was found to cause irreversible birth defects.

9. Stress? Yes, we all have stress. Life is stressful. I'm not asserting that my stress is any worse than anyone else's. But each of us handles (or doesn't handle) our stress uniquely. There is certainly no question that stress impacts our physical health.

Here are the particular stresses that affected me before my diagnosis:

In January 2008, my mom died. We weren't all that close, and our relationship was, shall we say, complicated. This may sound cruel, but when I knew that she was going to pass, I thought I might experience some relief. Well, I did experience some. What I didn't anticipate was that her death would hit me like a ton of bricks. It was much more difficult emotionally than I imagined it would be.

A few months after my mom passed, the recession hit the United States, devastating my business and most people who had any affiliation with real estate. Before the recession, my company had 90 employees and six offices throughout California. Over the next two years, I was forced to lay off all but six employees while also dealing with an angry bank who sued me over an outstanding $1.3 million credit balance. Over the next few years, we paid back every penny owed, something which I remain extremely proud of.

And during the recession, my marriage was falling apart.

So, yeah. All of these events were pretty fucking stressful. My friend, Michael O., seeing how stressed I was during this period, would often remind me, "Keep track of your health."

I'm not sure I did.

At the end of the day, I'll never know how I got a big tumor in my pancreas. But thinking about the possible explanations helped shape my plan going forward. I would be more mindful about stress, watch my diet, exercise regularly and focus on the things I could control rather than the things I could not. I would also try to accept that I wouldn't do it perfectly.

THIRTY-ONE

Serendipity

Two days after returning from Germany, I resumed natural immunotherapy treatments every weekday for about four hours at Dr. Gisler's office in West Los Angeles. My health insurance didn't pay for any of the non-Western medicine treatments and it wasn't cheap. Thankfully, I still had a few thousand dollars left from the GoFundMe Germany money to help.

Over the next six weeks at Dr. Gisler's office, I received regular infusions of high-dose vitamin C, glutathione, ozone and thymus injections. At home, I was injecting mistletoe into my abdomen and performing regular coffee enemas.

Back when I was doing chemo, I'd visit once a week for an hour or two, and then feel shitty for several days at a time. This "alternative" approach was much more time-consuming. In addition to spending on average four hours every weekday at Dr. Gisler's, I practiced yoga and meditation at home, which took another hour. I was also working full-time, parenting, doing my best to be a good boyfriend and trying to have a life.

In mid-May, I reached out to the cancer clinic at Stanford University to inquire about the immunotherapy clinical trial that the researchers at Johns Hopkins had approached me about a couple of days before I left for Germany.

Eventually, I got this response:

The drug we are using (pembrolizumab or Keytruda) has just been approved by the FDA across the board for MSI-high tumors, so you should ask your local oncologist about it and see if you can get it locally.

I did a quick Google search and found this:

The U.S. Food and Drug Administration today granted accelerated approval to a treatment for patients whose cancers have a specific genetic feature (biomarker). This is the first time the agency has approved a cancer treatment based on a common biomarker rather than the location in the body where the tumor originated.

Keytruda (pembrolizumab) is indicated for the treatment of adult and pediatric patients with unresectable or metastatic solid tumors that have been identified as having a biomarker referred to as microsatellite instability-high (MSI-H) or mismatch repair deficient (dMMR). This indication covers patients with solid tumors that have progressed following prior treatment and who have no satisfactory alternative treatment options and patients with colorectal cancer that has progressed following treatment with certain chemotherapy drugs.

Needless to say, this was a very pleasant surprise. Now I just had to find a new oncologist.

THIRTY-TWO

Dr. Wainberg

As excited as I was to continue my health journey on this very different path, I remained exhausted, sometimes sad and often angry. I was still going through bouts of depression, with occasional thoughts of suicide. I was obsessed with healing, but also obsessed with possibly dying. Obsessions can be healthy or hurtful, sometimes both. All I knew for certain was that I was crying a lot while trying to keep it together. It often felt impossible.

I wasn't the greatest parent during this period. I often question and second-guess my parenting anyway, but during the first few months of my cancer journey, I became obsessive about this.

I didn't talk a lot about my situation with my kids. They could see when I was struggling (mostly with fatigue), but I kept my crying spells mostly to myself.

In my despair, I would convince myself that everyone was moving on without me. Susie was starting to thrive in her new real estate sales career, my kids were living their lives and I was alone struggling for my life.

I would make myself feel very alone.

Susie, who could see that I was in the thick of it, was there to remind me I wasn't alone. After we learned that the FDA had approved Keytruda for my rare condition, Susie reached out to the UCLA Oncology Department (very close to my house in Santa Monica) and to the City of Hope in Duarte (which might as well have been in another state it was so far away).

When you live in Southern California, the prospect of spending too much time in an automobile can influence life decisions. There wasn't any way I was going to Duarte. Plus, it didn't matter which facility I chose; they were administering the same treatment. I wasn't too concerned at that point about finding the "right" oncologist because, by this point, I had become the CEO. I could make the decisions.

On May 30, Susie and I met with a possible new oncologist, Dr. Zev Wainberg, and his nurse practitioner, Megan Price. Dr. Wainberg is in his 40s, a couple of inches shorter than me and has a matter-of-fact demeanor. Dr. Wainberg needed more data before proceeding so blood work and scans were scheduled over the next three weeks. Once the tests were completed and insurance was approved, I was tentatively scheduled to start immunotherapy in late June.

But there was another hurdle to navigate before starting the new treatment. On June 23, while driving, I saw just the first line of an email on my iPhone from Megan Price:

Unfortunately, the insurance company does not cover this drug under your benefits.

I was livid. My thoughts raced from anxiety to anger. What the fuck were they talking about?

Then I read the rest of the email:

However, the form attached will help us get this drug approved and started. We do have it in stock, so as soon as we get the green light from Merck, who supplies the drug, we can get started. We will make sure you are still able to receive this treatment.

Whew! Basically, Dr. Wainberg was having me enter into an agreement with Merck, the maker of Keytruda, so the fees for the drug would be waived.

The content of this email was a reminder about how our twisted health care system works. If I wanted the Keytruda immunotherapy, I would have to play by their rules.

My reaction to this email was a reminder of how my emotions could swing from dark to light so dramatically. I was down, I was up, I was angry, I was crying. I was all over the place. Emotional fluctuations had become a significant component of "The New (Ab)normal." When you get diagnosed with a serious form of cancer, it can surround and dominate your life.

THIRTY-THREE

A Bad Coincidence

Larry DuBois and I met in 1968 at Madison Junior High School in the San Fernando Valley. I liked Larry and the group of kids he hung out with, but we weren't close friends. Years later, I started working as a box-boy at Dale's Market in Van Nuys. On my first day, I was happy to see that I knew someone else who worked there: Larry from junior high school!

Larry and I quickly bonded over everything from music to sports to gossiping about our fellow employees and the strange customers who walked into the store. And, of course, we talked about the girls we were almost always too shy to approach.

We were pretty much inseparable for the remainder of high school and through college at Cal State Northridge. We went to dozens and dozens of concerts and music festivals, and on several trips throughout California. We went backpacking in the Sierras, camping in Yosemite and driving through various parts of California and Nevada.

What did I teach Larry? I taught him how to smoke pot. What did Larry teach me? He taught me how to be myself. Larry seemed more comfortable in his own skin than I was at that time. Watching how he treated himself and other people greatly contributed to my maturation process.

We've now been close friends for nearly 50 years. Larry was best man at both of my weddings; I was best man at his wedding. Even though Larry has lived in Northern California for almost 40 years and I'm a lifelong Southern Californian, we've managed to stay close through occasional visits or vacations, and regular phone calls, emails and texts.

During a phone call with Larry in 2013, he told me that his wife, Karen, wanted him to see a doctor about his forgetfulness. Larry was very defensive in relating this to me. He insisted that he was fine. Trying to be the supporting friend, and honestly not noticing anything at the time, I agreed with him that he seemed fine to me.

In April 2015, Larry, Karen and I met in New Orleans for their very first Jazz Fest. They were excited about learning the ropes from me, an old hat, and I was happy to be their tour guide. Together, we rented an Airbnb in Tremé, a historic neighborhood.

Inside the house, we went to our respective bedrooms and started to unpack. A few minutes later, Larry walked into my room and asked, "When did you get into New Orleans?" At first, I thought he was joking, since they had just picked me up from the airport 90 minutes before.

He wasn't joking. He caught himself a few long seconds later and remembered what had actually transpired. I could see Larry was both uncomfortable and a little embarrassed about our conversation.

What I saw that day, and what Karen had seen a couple of years before, was that Larry was in the beginning stages of early-onset Alzheimer's. He was diagnosed with the disease just a few months after I received my cancer diagnosis in October 2016. As of this writing, he's now at stage five of the seven stages of Alzheimer's.

My conversations with Larry are different now. It's mostly me carrying the conversation and also trying to interpret what he is attempting to tell me. I can still make him laugh, though, particularly when we talk about the escapades of our past. Sometimes when I call him, he'll talk for a few minutes, get flustered with his memory issues and hand the phone to Karen.

It was and remains remarkable to me that we are both simultaneously battling life-threatening afflictions. Talk about life throwing curveballs. The two Valley boys who a few decades earlier got stoned at rock concerts, back-packed, camped and traveled, young and carefree, could definitely not have imagined this.

THIRTY-FOUR

Fuck Cancer

On June 9, 2017, my older son, Jasper, graduated from John Adams Middle School in Santa Monica. It was wonderful seeing him after the ceremony with his friends, watching him smile and laugh.

With the joy, there was also some sadness. At the graduation ceremony, I ran into a few of the parents I knew, and from many I got the pity look. It remained tough, even many months after my original diagnosis. Everyone meant well; they were just showing concern. But I didn't want to be the focus of anyone's attention unless I chose to be. And having cancer wasn't a choice.

As I watched Jasper graduate, I was wondering, *Will I be around in two years to watch AJ graduate middle school? Will I be around in four years to watch Jasper graduate high school?*

Having cancer was a stark reminder that when it comes to life, there are no guarantees. Any of us can walk out of our homes and get hit by a car. Or be killed by a terrorist. Or contract a deadly virus.

When you have a serious illness, the internal voices are

louder, the questions and fears are bigger and it can dominate your thoughts, even in the happiest moments.

* * *

Although I was still working and parenting full-time, at
night the loneliness would creep in. Susie and I did not live
together, so my loneliness was especially bad on the alter-
nating weeks I didn't have the kids. Those weeks, it was just
me and Max, my golden retriever.

I would try watching cable news, but it was all Donald
Trump all the time, and that made me nauseous and angry.
And it was hard to watch television anyway because of all
the pharmaceutical company ads. There were tons of
cancer drugs advertised, which was something I'd never
paid attention to before being diagnosed.

I also became attuned to what people on social media
were saying about cancer. I would get hung up on
comments like these:

He's battling cancer.
He lost his courageous fight against cancer.
She lost her valiant battle with cancer.
She's fighting cancer.
Fuck cancer.
Fuck that bitch cancer.

These comments made me want to think about a
different way of describing my situation. I felt that it was
too much energy to fight or battle with anyone or anything,
let alone something inside your body that can kill you.

I preferred to think of cancer as a very talkative,
obnoxious roommate who doesn't clean up after himself.
He has an element of danger to him, and you're not really

sure if you can trust him. He could erupt without warning. Heck, he might even burn the damn house down. And he's extremely difficult to evict.

Susie and I coined the phrase "making cancer fun," so we could laugh at the absurdity of it all. When we weren't feeling well, we'd say, "Could be cancer." Have a headache? Must be cancer. Unexplained fatigue? Cancer. A strange, small growth on your skin? Cancer. Making cancer fun and making fun of cancer helped me to remember that life could be lighthearted.

THIRTY-FIVE

Starting Keytruda

Later in June 2017, I had another appointment with Dr. Wainberg and Megan Price. The results of the scan were good, at least as *they* defined the word "good." The cancer had not grown or spread since January, which I interpreted to mean that the non-traditional path I had taken had, at the very least, kept things at bay.

My sense was that oncologists are thrilled when cancer doesn't grow or spread. I didn't experience anything close to thrill. To me, it was just a feeling of relief. I was still alive and headed in a better direction. I just wanted this damn thing out of my body completely.

Dr. Wainberg and Megan informed me that I was good to go for a two-year immunotherapy treatment program. Dr. Wainberg felt that I should put most of the non-traditional modalities on hold while I was receiving the Keytruda and my other doctors agreed.

My first immunotherapy appointment was at the UCLA Santa Monica clinic just a couple of miles from my house. The plan was to get an infusion once every three weeks, with scans to measure progress about every four months. The infusion itself was quick—30 minutes. It took another hour for the nurses to draw blood and to get lab results back before administering the drug. The entire process was easy-peasy.

After the first treatment, the side effects seemed to be minimal. I felt some discomfort in my stomach and my digestion was a bit off; it was nothing compared to chemo.

Over the next few weeks, I started living my life again. I was working more, getting out at night more and more active in general.

It wasn't just the treatment that helped me. It was also the support. A few weeks earlier, I'd met with my friend and "spiritual adviser," Brad, in Coronado. I had a change in perspective on this trip. I realized I hadn't been actively participating in my life; instead, I'd been mostly watching it.

After my bad experiences with Dr. Lester and the doctor who recommended me to him—the one who had advised me to pray—I was now surrounded by people in the medical and healing communities who I liked and trusted. I had love from my kids and from Susie. And every day, I would receive either messages, emails, texts or calls from people expressing their best wishes for me. I was a lucky guy.

* * *

Later that summer, while sitting in a coffee shop in Santa Monica, I ran into Julie B., a school parent who I hadn't seen for a couple of years. She asked me how I was doing. With people I hadn't communicated with for a while, I never knew if this question was a pleasantry or if it was about cancer.

It turns out Julie did know because she'd been tuned in

to my blog. And she was so gracious and kind, so much so that I had to bite my lip. I wasn't about to cry at Starbucks!

Also that summer, I started receiving calls and messages from people who'd heard about my story through other people or Facebook. Generally, these people fell into two categories: friends or loved ones of cancer victims and fellow cancer victims themselves. Those who were suffering from cancer also fell into two categories: those who had received a recent diagnosis and those who weren't doing well with their current treatment regimen. Many of these people asked for my advice and wanted to learn more about what I had done in Germany.

I was happy to talk with anyone and everyone. But what I would always tell people was this: I can't give any medical advice. I'm not a doctor, and every situation is different. Also, my health status was a work in progress. Yes, I was feeling better, but I had no way of knowing if it would stay that way. Instead of giving advice, I shared my experience. And perhaps I was giving other cancer patients some hope.

To date, about 75 people have asked me about my cancer story. Sadly, some of the cancer patients I spoke with are no longer with us. Each time I hear the sad news of someone's passing, I remember how fortunate I am to still be alive.

THIRTY-SIX

Work

In one form or another, I had been in business for myself since 1987, when I was 30 years old. My consulting company mostly worked for real estate developers, preparing environmental impact reports to predict the effects of their projects before they were approved and built.

For the first six years, I had a partner, Jim Brock. At the start, Jim and I probably knew as much about running a business as two kids operating a corner lemonade stand.

After building a business with about 10 employees, I realized I didn't have the right personality for a business partnership, and Jim and I parted ways in 1993. After I left, I became a true sole-practitioner, working completely on my own from my house in Santa Monica, well before telecommuting was a "thing." I remember back then being asked by many, "How can you work from home? Aren't you distracted?" My answer was always simple and direct. "If I don't work, I don't make money."

In 1995, I hired my first employee, Andy. Three more employees were hired after that, and I converted my garage into an office in 1997 for all of us. One thing led to another, and over the next 11 years, my company grew into six offices throughout California with a total of 90 employees.

It was wildly successful and I was making a boatload of money, but around 2007, I was extremely unhappy. The company's large size meant that much of my time was spent managing employees rather than helping our clients navigate successfully from Point A to Point B. I hated managing dozens and dozens of people. It felt like being a glorified sitter for adults. I started resenting going to the office every day.

Around the same time, my marriage started to fall apart. So going home wasn't much fun, either.

Then the recession hit in late 2008. I went from successful and unhappy to far less successful and crazy-miserable. Over the next two years, we were forced to downsize and close all but one office and lay off dozens and dozens of employees.

With just six employees, I rebooted the company in August 2010.

And I was instantly happier.

I'm proud that over the next several years, we built the company back up. Opportunities to grow the business presented themselves again, but I knew based on experience that I was not cut out to run a company of more than 10 employees.

While I was undergoing treatment for the cancer, I continued to work. But I was distracted by both the time my treatment was taking (at least until I started the Keytruda) and also all of the worrying and fear. I was lucky that the same group of employees who stayed with the company in 2010 were still working with me. They clearly picked up the ball when I couldn't.

By the summer of 2017, I dove back into work more fully. I was attending meetings again, something I had mostly avoided because I didn't want to encounter "the pity look" any more than I already had.

That July, I attended a meeting with the Department of City Planning at Los Angeles City Hall, a "bidder's conference" to discuss the parameters of the department's desire to change the way consultants were allowed to do work in the city. It was an extremely important potential change in how we would be able to operate and do our work.

It was wonderful running into my fellow consultants and city planners, many of whom I'd known for decades. As always, everyone was happy to see me; and showered me with kind words. In a way, it felt like a homecoming.

Given that our firm had done more work of this type than any other, I figured it was a slam dunk that we would be placed on the city's new list of "qualified consultants."

I had no idea that 18 months later, the city's flawed process would almost derail my company.

THIRTY-SEVEN

One-Year Anniversary

In mid-September, I went in for another CT scan to check on the status of my tumor.

It was agonizing to wait one to two weeks for the results.

It was torture.

As usual, I used the time to think about how I was going to die soon. Susie called my thought process "As The Neurotic World Turns."

It turned out to be a pivotal scan. The last two scans in April and in June had shown no growth of the tumor and no spreading. I presumed that this was because of my "alternative" treatments, and maybe because of all the other efforts I'd made to live more mindfully and healthfully.

"Mr. Joseph, the tumor has shrunk 20 percent."

Susie was with me when Dr. Wainberg told us the news, and to see her eyes light up and her face smiling so happily made me cry. Later that afternoon, I told my kids. AJ didn't say much, but I could see his eyes tearing up. That said it all.

On October 31, 2017, my one-year anniversary of being diagnosed with cancer, I was not just alive; I was doing well. That night, I attended Game 6 of the World Series, the Los Angeles Dodgers against the Houston Astros at Dodger Stadium. I was still working. Still loving Susie and my boys with all of my heart. I was also still struggling with occasional fatigue, depression and fear.

So much had happened in the last year: the rocky first few months, the chemo, the learning that my "garden variety" cancer was actually not that at all, the new diagnosis, going to Germany and coming back home. I was humbled by the journey, and more, by what it had taught me about love, devotion, friendship and loyalty.

As I wrote in my blog that day:

"Life is quite the ride, my friends. Let's hope there is a whole lot more."

THIRTY-EIGHT

Songs That I Sang in the Shower

My favorite place to cry was in the shower.

Seemingly every day, my routine was: wake up (often before 5 am), have a bowl of oatmeal for breakfast, do some yoga or meditation or exercise on a bicycle for an hour and then hop into the shower. The shower was my private sanctuary.

It must have been some combination of the heat on my skin, the steam and the relaxing nature of water that made me feel I could let my guard down.

Every single morning, I would break into tears. I sobbed, sometimes uncontrollably. Sometimes I cried so deeply that my body would heave. I would have to get down on my knees and brace myself.

I've been a crier since I was a little kid. Whether it was throwing tantrums (and for that my family nicknamed me Crabby Appleton, from the old *Tom Terrific* cartoon series that ran on the *Captain Kangaroo* show) to crying when I hurt myself, I was never shy about shedding tears as a young boy.

My easy willingness to cry followed me as a teenager

and into adulthood. If a girl broke up with me, I rarely got mad; instead, tears would flow. Even if I broke up with someone, I either felt so bad about the breakup or missed the girl (or both) that I would often cry.

And to paint the picture a little more clearly, two of my all-time movies are *Ordinary People* and *Terms of Endearment*, both tearjerkers. I often gravitate toward sadness and struggle in my musical tastes, from Bruce Springsteen's "Tunnel of Love" to Allison Moorer's "Blood" to John Hiatt's "Bring the Family" to Cidny Bullens' "Somewhere Between Heaven and Earth" to Jason Isbell's "Southeastern." All of these albums make me cry.

After my cancer diagnosis, I cried mostly out of fear.

I would start doubting my treatment program, and that would lead me back into the rabbit hole:

I will be dead in three months. I won't see my kids as adults. I won't get the chance to spend time in my later years with Susie after we're both empty-nesters.

Additionally, I always kept the bleak survival statistics for pancreatic cancer in the back of my mind. That was an unwanted but almost constant companion to my thought process.

That said, I had to constantly remind myself that there was zero evidence that I would be dead in three months. Or six months. Or five or 10 years.

Still, I cried.

Even when I got good news, I remained scared. Living in fear was exhausting. Sometimes I felt that instead of swimming, I was treading water for hours on end. I was like a shark. If I didn't keep moving, I would die.

I pressed on. What choice did I have? These thoughts of fear were my demons, my constant companions. Like cancer, I felt like I had to live and find a way to co-exist with them.

I also wasn't blogging much during the first few months of 2018. I was tired of hearing my own voice, tired of telling people what I was going through and feeling that I had said all I needed to say.

In mid-April 2018, I went to the French Quarter Festival and the Jazz and Heritage Festival, both in New Orleans. I had missed these festivals in 2017 since I had been in Germany for treatment. I had missed my friends, my New Orleans family.

It was both joyful and difficult.

I can't say I've had that many experiences in my life that I could describe that way.

Let me explain.

I soaked up the love, the thanks, the goodwill, the long hugs, the best wishes, the prayers, the "seeing you here made my French Quarter Fest" words. It was really amazing. I mean, really amazing.

As I talked to people and listened to what they had to say, I also ached emotionally. I turned away to cry. I stopped myself in mid-sentence several times because I was afraid the crying wouldn't stop.

At times, I wondered if I was attending my own memorial service.

At times, I wondered if I could continue walking down this path with dignity.

At times, I wondered how much longer I could even walk this path.

My friend, Paul Sanchez, invited me to sit on the side of the stage for his set at Jazz Fest that year. And when he performed "Life is a Ride" and told the origin story of the song, I was simultaneously thrilled, humbled, surprised and honored to look out into the audience and see a few hundred people mouthing the words to the song that I had helped create.

THIRTY-NINE

Hike Pie Toy

I continued getting my immunotherapy treatments every three weeks, and in May 2018, almost halfway through the two-year program, I went back in for yet another CT scan.

Yet again, the waiting was torture.

Even though this time the wait was only three days, I went straight to the darkest places possible in those three days. *I'm not going to see my kids grow up* was always my first thought.

I did not get bad news.

There was an additional 10 percent shrinkage since the last scan, bringing the total to 30 percent since I had quit chemotherapy in March of the previous year.

The doctor continued to be thrilled.

I was...relieved. And happy. And did I say relieved? My worst fears were not coming true. I was getting to see my kids grow up.

* * *

Ever since my first son, Jasper, was born in October 2002, I stated my desire (without much dissent from Carmen, my then-wife) that we continue our adventure travels. Carmen and I had traveled to New Zealand in early 2001, just a few months after we had met, and in November 2001, we went to Nepal and Thailand for our honeymoon. Less than three months after Jasper was born, we ventured off to Kauai.

Travel and adventure were in my blood, and it was something I wanted to expose my children to when they were really young. Over the next few years, we took several family vacations to Hawaii, spent two weeks in Tuscany and went on various trips throughout the continental United States.

And then there were the Sierras.

My dad used to take my brother, Jeff, and I and some-times a couple of our friends or extended family members to Yosemite almost every year until my mid-teens. Being in Yosemite almost every year amidst fresh air, granite, flora and fauna, rivers and streams, waterfalls, hiking trails and deep blue skies seeped into my blood—into my soul.

After I got my driver's license when I was 16, my friends and I would continue my annual tradition of going to Yosemite, sometimes twice a year. There were very few years that I missed driving up there and seeing my favorite place in the world.

And my visits to Yosemite almost every year continued for the next three decades, whether it was going with a friend, a group of friends, girlfriends or my wife.

It was a tradition I wanted to continue with my children.

And so I did. We took Jasper to Yosemite and Mammoth Lakes when he was just a toddler in the early 2000s, and at one point, Carmen and I purchased a vacation cabin in Mammoth, just a hop, skip and a jump from Tuolumne Meadows in Yosemite. The annual trips to the Sierras continued, sometimes multiple trips in the same year.

After Carmen and I split up in 2011, I continued the tradition of bringing the boys to the Sierras and Yosemite in the spring and to Mammoth and Yosemite in the summer. It was a family tradition that continued even after my cancer diagnosis.

Our summer Sierra trip in 2018 marked the ninth anniversary of "Hike Pie Toy."

Nine years prior, I knew I had to pull something out of my bag of parental tricks to get the boys to go hiking with me. I would always make the hikes easy, and I would insist that they go, but there were plenty of times I was gritting my teeth while they moaned and complained.

They had hiked many times before the advent of Hike Pie Toy. Back when Jasper was two and AJ was still a baby, I took them to Tuolumne Meadows in Yosemite and distracted them by teaching them how to count in French: "*Un, deux, trois, quatre, cinq.*"

And then I would blurt out, "Poop!'

That worked as a distraction on hikes for a couple of years. And then it didn't.

Little kids generally don't want to take long walks. And my boys would often resist my early attempts to take them hiking, though I would plow right through their objections with thoughts to myself like, "You can be miserable at home or you can be miserable on vacation." Hike Pie Toy was essentially an idea that I pulled out of my ass to bribe my kids to hike with me. They were four and six at the time.

Based on the memorable three-word title of Elizabeth Gilbert's memoir *Eat Pray Love*, I invented Hike Pie Toy. I might have called it for what it was, Hike Bribe Boys. But that seemed a bit too direct.

The deal with my sons would be as follows: as part of our annual summer trip to the Sierras, we would set out early in the morning for a drive to Mosquito Flats at the end of the road past Rock Creek Lake, about a 30-minute drive from Mammoth Lakes.

The Mosquito Flats trailhead elevation was about 10,000 feet, but the hiking was relatively easy for children, with only slight elevation gains. The hike generally took about 90 minutes, and we would stop halfway at a stunning scenic overlook where we could look down below at a lake and all around us and see the magnificent snow-capped peaks. We would take turns looking at a particular piece of scenery that caught our eye and then describe in a sentence or two why we liked it or what it meant to us.

After the hike, it would be off to Pie in the Sky, the restaurant just a stone's throw from Rock Creek Lake and a couple of miles from the Mosquito Flats trailhead. The owners of Pie in the Sky baked some of the freshest and tastiest pies in the world.

And then, for many years, it was off to a toy store in Mammoth, usually to buy some Legos.

By the summer of 2018, the boys were too old for toys.

And on that visit that July, they didn't even want the pie.

But they still wanted to do Hike Pie Toy—even though it was just Hike. They looked forward to hiking now.

After this trip, AJ said, "Hiking and being in nature is now in our blood." And he thanked me.

FORTY

Two-Year Anniversary

My two-year anniversary of being diagnosed with third stage pancreatic cancer was rapidly approaching that October 2018. I was anticipating that day with my usual mix of awe that I was still alive, gratitude that I was still improving and my constant companions of fear and anxiety. I still had this unwanted roommate in my body that, though it was getting smaller, refused to leave.

In early September, I got another CT scan.

Because I'd had had so many scans by this point, I knew the drill and could even joke about it. As usual, I arrived an hour early to sip my cup of the milky barium "drink" four times at 15-minute intervals before they brought me into the scan room. The fluid is a contrast dye used to examine a specific part of the body by making it appear opaque. I joked with Susie that my happy hour cocktail was delicious (it wasn't) and that she should join me in the festivities. She didn't.

Once in the room, I laid down on the table that looked like a truncated MRI machine. Happily, this meant no claustrophobia. After the technician injected more contrast fluid into my arm, the table was moved into the tube so that my abdomen and chest could be scanned.

The scan itself took maybe 10 minutes.

Now, I get that I'm not a VIP, a politician, a rich person or a celebrity. And I also know that a radiologist has to look at the scan results first, write a report and send it to my doctor. I get that that all takes time.

However, when I was diagnosed with cancer two years before, I received that bad news directly from a radiologist within about 30 minutes of having my scans performed. Thirty minutes!

Getting the results of the September 2018 scan took nine days.

Nine long "I'm so sorry to tell you this, Mr. Joseph" days.

I wrote my obituary in my head a dozen different ways. I fantasized that people would remember me fondly, then quickly forget that I had ever existed. It was self-inflicted torture. I wasn't just visiting a dark place in my mind. I was living there.

The results were really good. My tumor had now shrunk to about two-thirds of the size it had been in March 2017, when it was its largest.

Dr. Wainberg and Megan were very pleased. I was relieved that I would finally get a good night's sleep.

FORTY-ONE

Capitol Hill and Other Hills

On January 1, 2019, my boys and I boarded a plane to visit Washington, D.C. It was their first visit to the nation's capital and I was so excited to show them the sights of a city that on my previous visits had always left me in awe.

We visited the Supreme Court Building, walked by the White House and took a tour of the Capitol Building on the same day that the new Congress was being sworn in. We soaked in the architecture and vibe of this historical city. Unfortunately, our six-day trip landed smack in the middle of the federal government shutdown, which meant we couldn't go to any of the Smithsonian museums.

Halfway into the D.C. trip, I received an urgent text from my office manager, Andrea, simply stating *CALL ME*. We were in the midst of doing our walking tour of the monuments, and I was trying to avoid work as much as possible to stay present. I figured whatever it was could just wait.

Later that same day, I checked my email and saw that Andrea had forwarded me an email with the message, *Please read!*

The email included a two-paragraph letter from the City of Los Angeles Planning Department stating that we had not been included in their list of qualified consultants to do work in the city. There was no explanation accompanying this decision.

If my jaw could have hit the floor, it would have burrowed a two-foot hole in the ground.

Aside from shock, I felt angry, surprised and hurt. Oh, and scared. My livelihood, my employees' livelihood and my ability to support my family were all immediately threatened. If this decision stood, I would be out of business. Plain and simple.

I was trying to take this all in and figure out how to respond while we were walking into the Martin Luther King Jr. Memorial. I thought, *I'm dealing with cancer, I'm trying to survive and now I have to fight for my livelihood? Are you serious?* I felt deflated and exhausted.

I needed a plan, but at that moment I had nothing.

Flying home a couple of days later with confusing thoughts swirling around in my head, I happened to be seated immediately next to what I presumed to be a married couple. They were scrolling through some photos on the husband's iPhone and talking about being at the Capitol Building for the congressional swearing-in ceremony. Since we had also been visiting at the Capitol Building that day, I struck up a conversation with them.

It turned out that they were the parents of new Congresswoman Katie Hill, a Democrat from the northern part of Los Angeles who had turned a longtime Republican seat into a victory for the Democratic Party in the November 2018 elections.

Her parents were so happy about their daughter's election and swearing-in and so proud to show me the photos. It was nice to be distracted from my own troubles on the flight home, but it was also a bit bittersweet, as talking with Congresswoman Hill's parents also tapped into my fear of not seeing my kids as adults like this couple had been able to do with their daughter.

A postscript to the Katie Hill story: you may know that her short congressional tenure did not go well. About 10 months after I had met her parents, Hill announced her resignation from Congress (coincidentally on October 31, 2019, my three-year cancer anniversary) because some past incidents in her private life appeared to have violated congressional rules. It was a reminder to me that not every story has a happy ending.

FORTY-TWO

You Can Fight City Hall

Dealing with a cancer diagnosis adds a huge layer of stress to one's life, way above and beyond the normal daily stresses of just living in this world. To try and deal with the potential death of my livelihood on top of that felt life-threatening with a few exclamation points added.

When I flew back to Los Angeles in early January, I really didn't know what I was going to do in terms of the matter with the municipality. What I did know was that I had mouths to feed: my seven employees (including me), Carmen (spousal support) and my two kids, and I was also helping Susie and her son, Milo, as Susie transitioned in her career.

I knew that if I didn't do anything to protest the city's decision, I could run out of money. As I had learned from my cancer journey, I could not be passive about this.

Andrea and Stacie in my office helped me draft an official letter of protest. That was a no-brainer. Beyond that, and because I had no idea why we had been rejected, I was scratching my head about what steps to take. Subsequent emails and calls to the city in January had yielded no information whatsoever on how they came to their decision.

In early February 2019, I reached out to my attorney friend, Gary, and asked him if he'd be willing to do an anonymous Public Records Act request for me. I needed more information. At that point, I didn't want the city to know I was sniffing around, but since we were more than qualified to make their list, I knew that something had to be going on for the agency to have reached its decision; either it was a mistake or something nefarious was happening.

My plan was that Gary would write the letter, we would obtain the information we requested, my staff and I would sort through it, and from there, we would figure out how to move forward. But a few weeks after receiving and reviewing the first batch of public records, I quickly realized we needed more information because we were only scratching the surface. Which meant additional Public Records Act requests. It was like being on a treasure hunt, except treasure hunts are supposed to be fun. This wasn't fun at all.

I had lunch in Santa Monica around the same time in February with Tom Clyburn, an attorney I'd worked with for more than 30 years. Tom wanted to pick my brain about internship opportunities in the environmental consulting field for his son who'd just graduated from college. After lunch, I walked with Tom back to his office to say hi to some other attorneys I knew at his firm.

I poked my head into the office of Bill Jenson, an attorney I hadn't seen in several years. Though it wasn't my intention, after a few minutes of conversation, I disclosed what was going on between my firm and the city and he took a keen interest in wanting to know more.

Up until that point, I had felt like I was fighting the city with one hand tied behind my back while walking in a very dark alley. I needed more help. I couldn't do this alone.

Within a week, I had officially retained Bill and Tom to help me fight this battle. They reviewed materials, ghost-wrote more Public Records Act requests under Gary's signature and, most importantly, provided thoughtful and strategic advice on how to move forward.

I also started talking with former employees of the city, many of whom were my friends. They gave me some insights as to why they thought this had happened. I used this information, plus the emails, reports and scoresheets that we received through the Public Records Act requests, along with Tom and Bill's advice, to help me determine what I thought at that time was the best course of action.

By gathering all the written and oral information, I learned why we had been rejected. For the purposes of the writing of this book, my attorneys have advised me to say as little as possible about what I found so as to not embarrass anyone. All I will write here is that the evidence we compiled showed that the city had made some "gross errors and mischaracterizations."

Over the next couple of months, my company submitted letters to the city, heavily documented and sourced, showing how they had misapplied their judgment criteria, had erroneously and unfairly judged certain firms and had made a mistake in not including our firm on their list.

In April, we received a letter from the agency denying our protest. I was even more shocked and angry than I had been when I received the news of our initial rejection in January.

It was time to escalate the battle and let the city know exactly that I wasn't going to roll over.

I huddled with Bill and Tom, and we decided to bring in a litigator to help fight our cause.

Meanwhile, I was still receiving my cancer immunotherapy treatments, still working full-time, still being a boss, still being a parent, still being a boyfriend and still trying to live life.

I was stressed out of my mind.

Sometimes you have to do what's right, even if it's costly financially, even if there is an emotional cost attached to it. Even if it's potentially costly to your health.

I knew I was right. I knew I had to plant my feet and fight. When I told Susie that I was "lawyering up," she responded by calling me a "badass" and saying that the city had no idea who they were getting into a fight with.

Bill and my new litigator, Dan, drafted a $10 million damage claim against the city, a necessary precursor to filing a lawsuit. The nearly 100 pages of attached documentation provided more than enough proof that the agency had erred in their decision.

It was the filing of the damage claim that finally got the attention of the agency, specifically their in-house city attorneys. The city attorneys reviewed all of the materials we provided and realized that their client (the agency) would lose if this ever went to court. Oh, and it would have been a huge embarrassment to them if this dispute went public.

Long story short, in August 2019, I was notified that we had won our case against the city, and our firm was added to the list of qualified consultants.

No, I didn't get the $10 million. And, yes, it cost me a bundle to pay my attorneys.

How does this relate to cancer?

I used the same playbook to deal with the agency that I had used to deal with my cancer treatment.

Take action. Take charge. Don't be passive. Question things. Enlist others to help. Do what you know is right. And know you can handle more than you think you can.

FORTY-THREE

Thoughts and Prayers

Thoughts and prayers. We see these words all over the news and on social media. This phrase is what we say after an atrocious event. And then it's mocked by those of us who don't consider "thoughts and prayers" to be an action item.

Throughout my cancer journey, many people have used some form of the phrase "thoughts and prayers." I even have two friends, Marianne and Patty, who early on were praying for me daily. A few times, we met for lunch and they prayed for me while sitting in my car outside the restaurant. Kurt, the pastor from Texas, would often send me texts offering prayers and warm wishes.

You may have gathered from earlier chapters that I'm not particularly religious. My parents were both Jewish, but they weren't at all religious. Religious Jews don't name their kid Chris. When I was a kid, I can't tell you how many times the parents of my Jewish friends would ask, "They named you Chris?"

Jewish holidays for me were just a day off from school. We never went to temple and never observed any of the holidays. As a teenager, I proudly proclaimed to anyone and everyone (even if they didn't ask) that I was an atheist. I just thought it was impossible that there could be a god. I would speak my mind about what I perceived as the inconsistencies in others' belief systems: is God all-knowing and all-powerful? Then how can we explain murder and disasters? Is God cruel? Apathetic?

I never received satisfactory answers to my questions. But I did feel morally and intellectually superior to those I asked, or at least that's what I was telling myself. I was also convinced that organized religion was the source of too many wars and human catastrophes over the centuries.

In my 20s, my belief morphed from atheism to agnosticism. Doubts had started to creep in about being a staunch atheist. After all, I couldn't prove there wasn't a god any more than someone else could prove that there was one. I began to feel that I couldn't commit to either side. I also modified my beliefs about organized religion: money and power were even greater contributors to human tragedy than organized religion. I remember an essay (and later a book) written by Charles Manson's prosecutor, Vincent Bugliosi, in which he wondered why God would get credit for good stuff in our world, but would escape blame entirely for anything bad that happened.

A couple of decades later, my thinking again changed, and it was heavily influenced by both having children and really appreciating the wonderment of nature. After my first son, Jasper, was born, I remember holding him and thinking, *How does this happen? How can we create children? This is a miracle!* I would go to the mountains nearby or to the Sierras and think, *Who created this? And why?*

I started entertaining the thought that maybe there was a god of creation, but he or she left the implementation to us. I still couldn't buy into the "almighty, all-knowing, all-powerful" paradigm.

In the last few years, I've realized that my opinions are not important. If there is a god, then what Chris Joseph thinks is irrelevant. And if there isn't a god, then what Chris Joseph thinks is irrelevant. I really don't give a shit whether there is a god or there isn't, and what I think doesn't matter anyway.

That's my religion.

I do believe in tolerance. In kindness. In fairness. In love. In giving. In sharing. In being a good person. In treating others the way you want to be treated. And I don't have to be religious at all to practice those beliefs.

My cancer journey has reinforced my belief that most people are kind, thoughtful, loving and tolerant, and I continue to be grateful to receive thoughts and prayers.

FORTY-FOUR

Patient's Bill of Rights

I completed my two-year immunotherapy treatment in May 2019. According to Dr. Wainberg, my immune system would continue to be boosted by the treatment it received, so theoretically after the two years, I would not need future treatment.

Dr. Wainberg was very up-front with the fact that doctors, scientists and researchers were still in the discovery stages of this treatment program; they would learn more as time went on. In other words, he wasn't guaranteeing anything. Not that he would or could anyway.

I had my next scan in August. The results? There had been no change to the tumor. It was the same overall 33 percent reduction; nothing had grown and nothing had spread.

During this appointment, Dr. Wainberg told me that he didn't know if the tumor would ever entirely go away, but that at this point it might just be comprised of dead cancer cells.

This information was a pleasant surprise to me. The only way to know for sure would be to have another biopsy, but that was a needlessly risky procedure and one that he did not want to undertake.

Susie and I walked out of the clinic and instead of just feeling relief, I actually felt happiness. I felt like it was the first time in almost three years that I had allowed myself to be happy over how my cancer journey had transpired.

I was very lucky. Pancreatic cancer kills a lot of people. Yet I was still here, alive and thriving.

I had stopped getting the pity looks, which was good. I was now on the receiving end of a lot of congratulations, high-fives and words of encouragement.

It had been almost three years into my cancer journey, and I was starting to feel like the Wile E. Coyote character in those old Looney Tunes cartoons. Wile would always find himself still alive after some incredible, tumultuous ordeal. Then he'd get over it fast. He'd brush himself off and continue on his merry way.

Somehow, after surviving a tumultuous, odds-stacked-against-me ordeal, I started to brush myself off and carry on in a merry way. I had learned that I possessed more will and endurance than I ever dreamed or knew I had.

I was still getting several inquiries from people who wanted to know my story. It was around this time, the "celebration" of my three-year anniversary, that I started jotting down notes about what I wanted to say. Call it a "Patient's Bill of Rights."

Patient's Bill of Rights:

1. You have the right to bring someone (a friend or loved one) with you to a doctor's visit. A friend or loved one will hear things you won't, and they will ask questions that you either don't

know to ask or are too scared to ask. It's also good for them to help with any note-taking. And to just be there for you.

2. Assuming your condition isn't immediately life-threatening, you have the right to obtain a second opinion. And maybe a third or a fourth opinion. You have the right to hear differing opinions (assuming there are some) and to consult with people who have gone the non-traditional route and with doctors and health practitioners who practice "alternatively."

3. You have the right to do your own research. Use the internet wisely to research whatever it is you are being diagnosed with. Remember to use a filter. Who is writing what you are reading and why? Are they being paid? If so, by whom? Remember to use critical thinking skills to help you decide if a claim or assertion is true, false, sometimes true and sometimes false or partly true and partly false. The internet is filled with misinformation. Doctors and medical professionals can also be dispensing misinformation.

4. Doctors aren't gods. They don't know everything. You have the right to find a doctor who admits they may not know something. Honesty and integrity go a long way.

5. You have the right to find a doctor who will sit with you and listen. Actually listen. Who will ask you questions. Someone who can look you in the eye and engage with you, rather than just dictate to you. Who will take more than 15 minutes with you.

6. Similarly, you have the right to find a medical

practitioner who will answer your questions. And you have the right to change doctors if your physician refuses to answer any of your questions or isn't willing to find the answers.

7. You have a right—and an obligation—to remember that what you put into your body has a direct impact on your health and on your ability to survive a cancer diagnosis. You have the right to ask your doctor about how dietary changes could impact your medical condition. Your doctor may or may not inform you of this.

8. You have a right—an obligation—to move your body to the extent that you can and to attempt to quiet your mind to help boost your immune system. Your doctor may or may not inform you of this.

9. When a doctor prescribes medication, you have the right to ask him or her about potential side effects. You have a right to ask your doctor about the potential side effects of the new medication in conjunction with any other medications you are taking. You have the right to review the warning label pamphlets that come with each medication. Unless you ask, doctors may or may not discuss these matters with you. And remember that medication isn't always the answer. Remember that because of television pharmaceutical company advertising (not allowed in most countries), Americans have become conditioned to wait for a magic pill or a vaccine. In addition to potential side effects, sometimes medication doesn't work. There could also be alternatives to medication. The current paradigm is that when we get sick, we

want the pills. Perhaps we can also ask how we could have prevented the condition from getting started. You have a right to ask about that.

10. Trust is earned, not given. You have the right to make your doctor earn your trust. Don't blindly trust someone just because they have the title "Doctor" in front of their name.

I wish I had known of all these things at the beginning of my journey.

Epilogue

The genesis of this book began innocently with the written and video blogs I started creating right after I was diagnosed with pancreatic cancer in October 2016. The idea to make my blogs into a book came about at the beginning of 2020 after dozens and dozens of people reached out to me wanting to know about my cancer journey. The blogs were a launching point for the book and comprised about a fourth of the raw material. They also served as a memory and fact-checking system. Without them, I don't know that the chronology and details of specific stories would have been nearly as accurate.

Coincidentally (or not), I put pen to paper (fingers to keyboard in my case) in March 2020, right when the COVID-19 pandemic hit the United States.

As I write this epilogue to my cancer journey, our country—our world—is still in the midst of a multi-pronged assault: a global health pandemic, an economic calamity, a pandemic of fear and changes to our way of living and to our society which, combined, none of us in the United States have ever seen. Simultaneously, we are seeing understandable and justified social unrest to try yet again to combat systemic racism, something that this country, in its 244-year history, has sadly not yet resolved.

Theoretically, I am in the "high-risk" category for COVID. I'm 63 at the time of this writing and have a serious underlying health condition. That said, the pandemic itself has not really moved my fear needle. Perhaps this is because after getting the surprise third stage pancreatic cancer news almost four years ago and having that scare the fuck out of me, I've become somewhat resilient. And perhaps it's helped me acquire some perspective on health matters.

COVID-19 is a virus. A deadly and tragic one, to be sure. But for me personally? I'd much rather take my chances on getting the virus than having to deal with pancreatic cancer. And the chances of getting the virus seem small. There are about 7.8 billion people in this world and only a very tiny percentage have contracted the virus. An even smaller percentage have passed away, sad as that is.

That's not to minimize in any way the tragedy that this virus has caused or to try and change anyone else's opinion as to how to feel or think about what this country—this world—is going through. It is a tragedy of epic proportions.

We hear very little about how unhealthy this country is and how that has contributed to the spread of COVID in the United States. That's not to excuse the federal response to this—plain and simple, it has been a major clusterfuck. But Trump is not responsible for the decline in the health of our citizenry. That's been going on for decades. And when you combine a very poor response to the virus with an unhealthy population, along with a medical system that ranks very low in industrialized nations and with the fact that we've been conditioned over the years to wait for a magic pill or a vaccine to cure us instead of focusing on eating healthier and exercising more—well, it's the perfect storm.

I long for the day when I hear an American politician, epidemiologist or a member of the media say to the public: "Hey, while you're waiting for a pill or a vaccine over the next one to two years, you might want to do what you can to eat healthier, move your body more and adopt better living habits." Our society can debate various strategies to lessen the effects of the pandemic like wearing masks, social distancing, shutting down the economy, etc., but there is no debate when it comes to getting healthier. We know that getting healthier and building our immune system work to help us from catching viruses and fighting them off if we do catch them. And there are no side effects from getting healthier.

But this book is not about me getting preachy and opinionated, even though I know I've already crossed that line a few times.

Plain and simple, this book is my story, my cancer journey. What worked. What didn't work. What I learned and experienced, the good, the bad and the ugly.

What I know is that I am still alive and doing pretty damn well through this rather unorthodox cancer journey. I know that chemotherapy didn't work for me and almost killed me. I know that the alternative treatments that I underwent both here and in Germany helped; how much, I simply don't know. The two years of Western medicine immunotherapy also helped; again, how much, I don't know.

I also know that eating healthier has helped. Moving my body every day has helped. Meditating has helped. Having a great support system, led by Susie and my kids, has helped. Thoughts and prayers have helped. Questioning my doctors and taking charge of my own health helped.

Still, I can't point to any one of these things and say that it's the reason I'm still alive. I might know a little. But there is a lot I don't know.

In closing, I'm going to answer three questions I get all the time:

Question 1: "How are you doing?"

Overall, I seem to be doing pretty well. My cancer situation is in check; nothing has grown or spread. I feel like I'm in good shape for a 63-year-old human, but an aging body and mind invariably suffer some decline. For the last few months, I've been dealing with some internal "tremors." Thankfully, doctors have ruled out Parkinson's or anything to do with cancer. I'm applying the same principles I've used in my cancer journey to treat the tremors. That means a lot of yoga and other forms of exercise, breathing and meditation, supplements and other alternative treatments. Pharmaceutical medication for me in most situations is a last resort.

I still get semi-annual cancer scans, and I still have ongoing fear that the cancer will rear its ugly head again. But I also try to remember that my cancer seemingly has the characteristics of a receding glacier.

Question 2: "How has this experience changed you?"

Cancer is a club that no one chooses to join. There was life before cancer, and life after. I was much more innocent and cavalier about life four years ago. I am more grateful than I used to be. I value things more. Seeing Susie smile and being with my kids makes my heart sing.

I cry a lot more. And I let people see the vulnerability. I don't care what anyone thinks about that.

I live in more fear, which I wish wasn't the case, but

I've learned to mostly accept it. Getting a cough is more than just a cough to me. Feeling what some consider to be a normal digestive pang is potential cancer to me. A headache to you is a theoretical brain tumor to me.

I don't think there will ever be closure. When you deal with a health crisis (or worse, the loss of a loved one), there is no such thing as closure. That said, I do believe in healing. And I am healing.

I've learned to cope. I continue to learn to deal with the adversity. I have learned what it means to be resilient. Jason Isbell, in a song about recovering from addiction, wrote, "It gets easier, but it never gets easy." That sounds about right.

Question 3: "How will you know when you beat cancer?"

You and I will both know that I've beaten cancer when I wind up dying from something else. Hopefully, that will be in another 30 years or so.

Meanwhile, I still cry in the shower almost every morning. I still think that every pain, every sensation I feel in my body, is somehow related to cancer. I still worry that I might be dead in three months, even though I'm now almost four years into this cancer journey, a journey that by all the statistics probably was not supposed to last this long.

I'm lucky. And grateful. I still get to laugh. I still get to seek and consume great music, movies and the written word. I still get to hike and vacation. I'm still running my company full-time, grateful that I'm surrounded by amazing employees who are loyal and hard-working to a fault.

I still get to hold Susie's hand and see her smile. Next year, I get to watch my oldest son, Jasper, graduate from high school. I'm also looking forward to seeing AJ graduate from high school in 2023. And to see Susie's son, Milo, graduate a few years after that.

A story doesn't end until it ends. Mine is still unfolding.

Chris Joseph, August 2020
#lifeisaride

P.S.: Writing this book wasn't and isn't about trying to make a ton of money or to become a best-selling author. It's an attempt to chronicle and make sense of my adventures with cancer and to offer hope and some tools for others who might be starting on a similar difficult journey.

I will be donating some of the net proceeds from this book to various charities that do a ton of good in this world. During the writing of this book, I reached out to two of the leading pancreatic research organizations in the United States to ask them if they wanted to mention the book to the readers of their newsletters. One organization did not respond. The other responded, but while they were happy for my outcome, they did not want to use their newsletter to publicize my book because I did not exclusively follow the conventional Western medicine path to treat my cancer.

Despite any misgivings these organizations may have about being associated with my story, they will still receive a portion of the net proceeds. They do good work and have saved lives.

Acknowledgments

I wish my parents were alive so they could read this book. I think they would have been proud. Thank you, Mom and Dad.

Thank you to my brothers, Jeff and Andy, for your love and support, even though you both still have ways of driving me crazy.

Thank you to my men's group, brothers of 25 years: Jordan, Jonathan, Michael, Todd, Rick, Matt and Daniel. You have helped me spiritually, mentally and emotionally more than you know.

Thank you to Paul Sanchez, and not just for the gift of your friendship. The bond we have created over the last 13 years was instrumental in leading to the song and this book. And thank you to all my other musician friends in New Orleans, especially to John Boutté, who taught me a life lesson about trust.

The hundreds and hundreds of Threadheads who I met in New Orleans from around the world would be too long to list here. But know that the saying we coined for ourselves, "Threadheads get shit done," also applies to the writing of this book. It would not have happened without the support of each and every one of you, and because of the experiences we shared together.

I'm blessed that I get to work with a group of top-notch humans who more than picked up the slack at my consulting business during my cancer journey. Thank you to Andrea, Stacie, Seth, Kerrie, Sherrie and Ryan.

Thank you to Julie G. for organizing the GoFundMe campaign and to the hundreds of people who donated to it for my Germany trip in 2017; and to Kurt, Mike, Jeff, Andy, Eugene and Ed for staying with me during my treatment time in Frankfurt.

A huge thank you to my health, medical and spiritual team: my therapist of 18 years, Pamela Varady; Dr. Melanie Gisler, my general practitioner; and Brad Willis, who wrote the foreword to this book. Also, a huge thank you to SportsFit Physical Therapy and the International Sportscience Institute for helping me get in much better shape.

When I started writing this book in March 2020, I joined an online daily writing group called Launch Pad Inner Circle, led by Emily Redondo and Anna David. Thank you to both of them and to the 28 members of this writing group: your honesty and authenticity inspired me every day. And thank you to Anna, Swan Huntley, Ryan Aliapoulios, Kaitlin Anthony and John Bialas of Launch Pad Publishing for helping me get this book out to the world.

Thank you to my former business partner, Jim Brock (Jim Brock Photography), for the cover photo and headshot.

Many of you don't know I was briefly married once before, in my early 20s. Colleen and I didn't work out as a couple, but she is one of the finest humans I've ever known. Coincidentally, she is also an oncology nurse and was more than generous in offering sage advice and good wishes over the course of my cancer journey.

To Larry, my dearest friend, who continues on with his own difficult health journey. Thank you for our five decades of friendship. And know that I think about you every day.

Thank you to Carmen for picking up the slack in parenting our boys during those days that I simply wasn't up to it. And thank you for fiercely loving our children. I always knew they were in good hands.

Thank you to Susie, my partner of the last eight years. Susie has loved me and held my hand throughout this journey, and has taught me about love, loyalty and devotion. Being able to talk, laugh and cry with someone I love is a gift beyond measure.

When my boys were much younger, I used to tell them almost every day: "I'm so lucky and grateful to be your Dad." I still feel that way. They inspire, teach and motivate me in ways that I simply cannot articulate. I love them deeply and unconditionally.

I firmly believe in the adage "It takes a village." This book would not have seen the light of day without literally hundreds and hundreds of people in my life. Thank you all.

My sincerest apologies to anyone I've forgotten.

About the Author

Over the last 33 years, Chris Joseph has started and managed three environmental consulting businesses, launched two fan-funded music record companies and founded a non-profit charitable foundation. He has also dabbled in philanthropy, songwriting and magazine writing, and he is currently studying for his real estate license. A Los Angeles native, Chris lives in Santa Monica with his two teenage sons and loves to spend time with Susie, his longtime girlfriend.

CPSIA information can be obtained
at www.ICGtesting.com
Printed in the USA
LVHW012311241020
669607LV00006B/480

9 781951 407292